grower gatherer

Edible perennials to forage in your garden

Jack Wallington

GREEN BOOKS
LONDON • OXFORD • NEW YORK • NEW DELHI • SYDNEY

GREEN BOOKS
Bloomsbury Publishing Plc
50 Bedford Square, London, WC1B 3DP, UK
Bloomsbury Publishing Ireland Limited,
29 Earlsfort Terrace, Dublin 2, D02 AY28, Ireland

GREEN BOOKS and the Diana logo are trademarks of Bloomsbury Publishing Plc

First published in the United Kingdom 2026

A catalogue record for this book is available from the British Library
Library of Congress Cataloguing-in-Publication data has been applied for

ISBN: HB: 978-1-3994-2685-5; ePub: 978-1-3994-2686-2; ePDF: 978-1-3994-2687-9

2 4 6 8 10 9 7 5 3 1

Designed by Austin Taylor
Printed and bound in China by RR Donnelley Asia Printing Solutions Ltd, Dongguan, Guangdong

MIX
Paper | Supporting responsible forestry
FSC® C144853

To find out more about our authors and books visit www.bloomsbury.com and sign up for our newsletters
For product safety related questions contact productsafety@bloomsbury.com

Contents

Introduction

Perennial edibles are easy-to-grow food plants and fungi that continue living from year to year. They provide food across the world at low cost or for free, and can usually be grown with minimal effort.

Our enduring love for perennial edibles

All plants, edible or not, can be categorised according to the way they live and die, which is helpful for growers for planning and understanding what to grow, when and where. Annual plants such as lettuce and peas germinate, grow, set seed and die in a year, while biennials like carrots produce leaves in the first year before flowering, setting seed and dying in the second year. Some plants called triennials do this over three years. Ephemeral plants, such as edible wildflower hairy bitter cress, grow, set seed and die within weeks or months, sometimes multiple times in one year.

With *Grower Gatherer* I hope to encourage everyone to explore the incredible world of perennial edibles, which are capable of living for many years. Most gardeners will already have some perennial edibles in their plot, even if they've never given them much thought. Good examples include fruit trees, and most herbs are perennial as well. Some perennials only live for three to five years, while others have been to known to survive for decades or even centuries. For instance, apple trees can live for more than 300 years in the right conditions. Many of the plants we grow as annuals are actually tender perennials too – such as tomatoes, which live for several years in their native, tropical climates but will struggle elsewhere without the help of a heated greenhouse or polytunnel.

There are many benefits to growing resilient edible perennials. Once established, most require very little physical work, making them ideal for anyone looking to create a low-maintenance space. Indeed, their deep root systems are less demanding of water, while mature plants are better able to compete with weeds and wildflowers by quickly outgrowing them in spring and summer, giving you less weeding.

Opposite A traditional orchard where animals and crops co-exist: the same principle applies to other uses in gardens with perennial fruit or nut trees.

Right A lovely wildflower, dandelions are important for early bumblebees. They are also very tasty for us – especially when fried in batter.

Unlike annual crops, you also don't have to sow perennial crops from seed every year, which reduces the number of spring jobs for the gardener. And if you do need more of a certain perennial crop, you can simply grow them from cuttings, divisions, rhizomes or stolons. These propagation methods usually result in mature plants in no time – or at least much faster than growing from seed.

Edible perennials are also far better at coping with challenging conditions. While small and tender seedlings are vulnerable to being eaten by wildlife, mature perennials have the energy to grow new leaves, or have stems and trunks that hold their leaves away from molluscs, rabbits and deer. Their extensive root systems are strong and stretch deep into the soil, giving them far better resistance to drought and heavy rainfall. As there is generally less need for digging (with the exception of root crops), the soil beneath perennial crops remains undisturbed, which improves soil structure. In conjunction with improved soil fertility from less disturbance, perennials will need less fertilising or none at all. As an added benefit, perennial roots bind soil particles, while living and fallen decomposing leaves shield soil from rain and run-off, which protects the soil from erosion. Decomposing and decomposed organic matter mixes with soil, helping it act like a sponge to further lock water into soil.

There are also plenty of environmental benefits to growing perennial edibles. For example, plants that come back every year in the same spot provide stable food sources for wildlife. This also includes life below ground where the soil is less disturbed. Worms, bacteria, protozoa and myriad other subterranean life forms improve soil fertility, helping plants grow strongly, but this requires undisturbed soil.

Below A grove of olive trees, *Olea europaea*, as part of a thriving wildflower ecosystem on the volcanic slopes of Mount Etna in Sicily. Olive trees can live for thousands of years.

As perennial plants grow, they also lock atmospheric carbon into their stems, trunks and roots through a process called carbon sequestration, part of photosynthesis. All life is made of carbon, and the more life there is in one spot, the more carbon it keeps out of the atmosphere. Fallen leaves left to decompose also lock carbon into soils as part of living soil systems, helping alleviate global warming.

There's another serious point to *Grower Gatherer* too. I want to add my voice to a growing conversation addressing the future of where our food comes from. To do this we need to first look to our past.

Evolving as we have from hunter-gatherers, it's time to pay more attention to the gatherer part of us. Foraging to find food grown naturally is in our DNA, and I believe it should also be in our gardens. It's not an original idea. Indigenous communities around the world today practise permaculture – permanent agriculture – because their ancestors grew crops in this way since time immemorial. It is, however, a radical idea to reject intensive growing and to return to nature-led practices, albeit through the lens of contemporary knowledge and technology.

We'll always need annual crops as part of our food mix, but it's time they budged over (sorry, annuals) to give perennial edibles time in the spotlight. They need to take centre stage in a movement towards the establishment of future-thinking, self-sustaining edible gardens.

Above Perennial edibles can be grown in mixed plant communities or traditional rows, such as grapes at this vineyard in Sicily.

Our time on Earth

Humans evolved as hunter-gatherers, and the term no doubt conjures images in our minds of early humans wielding spears, hunting and chasing prey. But what about the second part of our ancient name? We are *gatherers* too.

For millions of years our ancestral species, collectively called hominins, picked fruit, roots and leafy plants for nutrition, and this continued throughout the hundreds of thousands of years that *Homo sapiens'* have existed. Plants are known to have formed a significant proportion of hunter-gatherer diets and evidence indicates that in temperate and tropical zones we likely ate more foraged plants than hunted meat. In fact, research suggests that on average globally, plants probably made up 65–80 per cent of hunter-gatherer diets, explaining why our diets are so reliant on plant nutrition today.

Over time, we also learned to be *growers*, understanding how plants grow and sowing seeds of the food plants we liked where we wanted. Around 12,000 years ago, that skill became the agricultural farming of crops, when we all stopped wandering the Earth as nomads and settled down as homemakers and growers. However in truth, when it comes to growing and gathering plants, of the seven million years of our evolutionary lineage, it's only in the most recent hundred years or so, with the invention of industrial farming and supermarkets, that we've forsaken the very activity we spent much of our time doing: *gathering*.

The simple action of reaching out to hold and pick food from a plant, to eat it fresh and for free, is something everybody should still be able to do. Modern life means it's not always possible; not everyone has the space to grow nor the time to do so alongside a job and family. To further put people off growing food, the annual vegetables humanity has focused on cultivating are generally more labour-intensive, requiring a huge amount of knowledge to juggle schedules and tasks.

I love growing vegetables and derive a lot of joy from the process, but there's no denying it's hard work. Sowing seeds throughout the year, potting seedlings on, watering them, planting them out, mulching with compost or feeding them, supporting them with sticks or canes, and protecting them from animals and insects, who also think they look delicious. Harvesting them, washing them, peeling and chopping, cooking and then, finally, eating them. A kitchen garden is non-stop – thank goodness for farmers!

Over the years, this has focused my mind on minimising the amount of work needed to grow food. I have tried to find growing methods and varieties of hassle-free crops that need less time and effort, both to grow and to gather. And I've tried to optimise every step, and to work out when to relax or break the rules.

I was asked to write about my research for four years in my 'Two Hours on the Veg Plot' column for *Telegraph Gardening*, in which I discuss running my allotment in around two hours a week. I then shared trials in my 'Hassle-Free Harvests' column for *Gardeners' World* magazine and a *Guardian* Masterclass. With each new season and article, I've researched and grown crops to make my life, and hopefully yours, easier. Many of these were perennial edibles. As a garden designer I've added countless different perennial edibles to more than 100 gardens, testing them in different hardiness zones and soils across Great Britain. Over the last five years, my partner Chris and I have cared for a small organic farm filled with perennial edibles in Yorkshire, England (H4 / -10 °C to -5°C) on an exposed slope, 300m above sea level. This book is a summary of a decade of research.

We face a number of enormous challenges around the world when it comes to feeding the human

Left The island of Madeira, in the North Atlantic Ocean, is one of many islands around the world where small farms are a way of life, filled with terraces of perennial crops including sugar cane and tropical fruits.

Right Young plants I grew for free, including cuttings of perennial kale (back left), *Salvia microphylla* 'Cerro Potosí' (back right), two globe artichokes from seed (left and right) and a division of oregano (front middle).

race. Global warming is already changing our seasons, making it harder to grow important edible crops in the British Isles and even changing *what* we can grow. In arid regions near the equator, it will likely become impossible to grow anything at all for many communities in the coming years as fertile land continues to desertify. Then there is infrastructure; with eight billion people reliant on only a handful of crops, including wheat, rice and corn, and the number of growers and suppliers decreasing, our food supply is vulnerable to unexpected natural, political and economic shocks. At the same time, industrial farming methods, such as poor management of soil and an over-reliance on artificial fertilisers, lead to erosion and strip away organic life and fertility, reducing the amount of quality land available to grow food.

Something must change. Big questions loom around how we are going to feed future generations of humans across the world, and how we will make sure everyone receives equal access to nutrition.

In other words, existential crises colliding with my laziness have focused my mind on possible solutions and one of them is *perennial edibles*.

Grower

When I was a little boy, my grandparents received a small amount of money for their retirement, but instead they generously gave that money to me, my sister and brother to each buy something special. I loved growing seeds and was lucky enough to use my portion to buy a small but real greenhouse. It was the most amazing place. I spent hours in there, sowing nasturtiums, tomatoes and courgettes. My dad showed me how to grow cuttings from succulents and my granddad fuchsias.

One day, and I'm not sure why I did this, I decided to plant a potato in the pot of my parents' beloved houseplant. As it sprouted, I added some dead leaves to the top of the compost, based on my basic understanding that leaves rot into soil, feeding plant growth in the woods behind our house. Thinking to myself then, wouldn't it be brilliant if the pot could be like that, fed by dead leaves that rot down in a never-ending natural cycle – with no other feeding from me nor anyone else, only plucking an occasional tasty potato to eat. I knew this wouldn't work, that the leaves would take months to decompose and it would take more than a few leaves, but my imagination hoped. A doomed experiment in more ways than one, my dream met its end with an angry shout from downstairs: 'Who planted a potato in the aspidistra?!'

Without realising, that was the start of a lifelong daydream of growing plants with minimal or no input from us. If nature can grow and flourish without us, why does it need so much input in our gardens? While it may sound like I was ahead of my time, I can assure you these ideas stemmed solely from a natural feeling of laziness and curiosity. Wouldn't it be better to grow without constantly adding stuff like fertiliser?

These days, such ideas are bogged down with jargon: permaculture, plant communities, forest gardening, regenerative growing, and so on. When really all we're talking about is ecology – the study of all living things and their environment – and applying it to edible plants. Or we could just call it *nature* – we need to find ways for crops to grow, provide food and nourish the soil in a natural cycle.

Fast forward 40 years and I've proven to myself through my design practice that it is possible to plan self-sustaining and low-maintenance plantings using plant community design (see page 13). For me, it was a small step to take this knowledge of designing ornamental plant communities and applying it to edible perennials. I'm not the only one; there are many gardeners, designers and food growers planting in this way around the world right now. Indigenous communities have always foraged and grown within permanent ecosystems.

Above Herbs and edible flowers can be very colourful. Shown are herb fennel (left), *Salvia microphylla* 'Cerro Potosi' (middle), *Agastache* 'Black Adder' (right) and chives (bottom).

Growing food is a fascinating subject: it's fun and pretty easy to get started. Even in tiny spaces we can grow something to eat, from an indoor windowsill to a balcony, to small plots of land or something a bit bigger. We can all grow food. Perennial edibles aren't new; they've been around forever, but by focusing on them we can grow more food more easily. And if we can grow the food, then we can all experience the primal joy of *gathering it*.

Gatherer

From the moment our first hominin ancestors evolved, we have loved food. Picking it, tasting it, stuffing our faces with it. Our brains are so big and clever, and our hands so dexterous, partly because of the way we used to forage for food. This steered us towards the evolution of senses to identify different plants, along with a big memory to store that information and communicate it across generations.

When I stand in our garden, the soft summer sun on my skin, and I pick a sweet, sun-warmed apple, or a leaf straight from a plant, I feel sad at how detached the world has become from gathering food. A century ago, my grandparents' generation all gathered food in various ways: fruit from a tree, herbs by the door. Today, most of our contact with food is in supermarkets and sealed behind plastic. In fact, many people fear picking from and eating plants because they haven't done it before. They are worried they may do something wrong or that the food may be dirty or unsafe.

As a food grower, I'm constantly harvesting food across the year. Like our ancient ancestors, I gather food almost every day from plants I've grown and from the wild. I wonder why growing edibles in our gardens and foraging are two different things, removed from each other in various ways.

Farming has freed us from time spent growing and gathering to concentrate on different jobs, creative pursuits, friends, family and relaxing. It's responsible for increasing human health and scientific progress. Yet, there is a part of me that says detaching ourselves from growing and gathering food entirely doesn't feel right – for the big-picture reasons discussed in this book but also because it is a part of who we are. Picking and eating plants is one of our strongest connections with the natural world that sustains us all. Plus, it's fun and a mind-focusing pastime.

Alongside wild foraging, growing perennial edibles is one of the easiest ways people can reconnect with food and re-engage with the gatherer part of our brains. Usually very low-effort to grow and beautiful, these perennials also help to remove the foraging fear barrier because they live from year-to-year, allowing us to learn to recognise them and how to use them in meals. They enable us to turn our outdoor spaces into living larders with plenty to forage when we feel like it, without adding to our lengthy to-do lists. I think of this as a forage garden.

Right Picking blackberries from our edible hedge which also contains sloes, elderflower, hazelnuts and crab apple.

How to plan a forage garden

Perennial edibles can be grown in regular rows, but the real fun begins when we experiment with growing them in a different way. Plant community design is when we regard planting areas as a whole entity, as well as a collection of individual plants. This allows us to plan planting areas with a varied and dense mix of different species in self-sustaining ways.

Your garden's conditions

Always start planning a new planting by considering the main factors that impact plant growth and the plants suitable for your garden. To do this, ask yourself the following questions:

- **Soil:** What type of soil do you have in your garden? Is it sand, clay, loam or a mix? How fertile is the soil and how much organic matter does it contain? How deep is the soil before hitting bedrock? Does the soil allow water to drain away freely or is it waterlogged? What pH is it?
- **Temperature:** What is the lowest temperature in the space? Plants have different thresholds for surviving cold temperatures and won't survive temperatures lower than their minimum threshold. If you live in a very hot region, the same is true for the maximum heat tolerance.
- **Water:** What is the annual rainfall? Is it high or low? Is your local water table high or low? Should you grow crops that need constant moisture in summer because you have reasonable rainfall, or do you need to focus on drought tolerance?
- **Sunlight:** Is most of your garden in full sun (direct sunlight all day), full shade (no direct sunlight), partial shade (direct sun for part of the day), or a mix of light levels? How does that change through the day and year? How will light change in future years (perhaps as a young tree or hedge grows)?
- **Space:** How big is your planting area exactly? How many plants can it accommodate at full size? Always plan to add plants according to their *final* growing size and compare this to your garden.

Opposite Our chickens happily free range in our edible perennial bed filled with large plants they can't reach, including herb fennel, coastal hog fennel, globe artichoke, *Salvia microphylla* 'Cerro Potosi' and perennial kale.

Sustainable composts

The best compost to use for seedlings or plants in pots is peat-free, made from a mix of composted bark and other plant material, and sometimes sheep's wool. Peat-free compost is water-retentive with a good, free-draining structure. It is also increasingly sustainable by using waste material from agriculture and forestry, whereas peat-based composts are dug from precious natural habitats, releasing carbon into the atmosphere that has been locked in bogs for thousands of years. When compost is mentioned throughout this book, it only refers to **peat-free** compost.

Making your own compost is relatively easy and can become addictive! Pile up dead plant material in a compost bay or a free-standing heap using a mix of about 40–50 per cent woody to 50–60 per cent green leafy material. Don't add seed heads or perennial weed roots that could grow. Try to add material in layers like a lasagne. Chop or shred large pieces of stem or twigs, so everything is only about 2–3cm long, to speed up decomposition. Shredded young branches of trees, such as from a clipped hedge or coppiced willow, make an excellent compost ingredient.

Over the course of a year, turn the pile two to three times to properly mix the outer material into the middle where it is hottest and decomposition happens the fastest.

Most pot-grown plants like ordinary peat-free compost but sometimes you may need something specialised. Plants labelled as being acid-loving need ericaceous compost, which means slightly acidic. Citrus fruits such as lemon are acid-loving but prefer compost specially formulated for citrus fruits. Both ericaceous and citrus compost is available peat-free.

When adding compost to soil outside as a mulch or to planting holes, any multi-purpose, peat-free compost is fine, although soil improver is probably better as it tends to be a bit cheaper. Soil improver is only suitable as a mulch – not pot growing – because it's a chunkier, slightly less decomposed compost that mixes well with soil.

Sowing and growing

Throughout this book I've included information on how to sow, grow and propagate each crop. However, there are some simple rules worth knowing:

- **Sowing seeds:** Always follow the packet instructions for timing, temperature, light and depth. As a rough rule, I tend to plant seeds with about as much compost or soil above them as their height. For instance, a nut is planted about 1–2cm deep, while dust-like chamomile seed is sown on the surface.
- **Moving and dividing plants:** This is generally best done in spring or autumn when the ground is warm and damp.
- **Cuttings:** These are usually best taken from spring to late summer when it is warm and there is lots of light.
- **Spacing:** Plants should always be planted according to their final size – don't be tempted to fill gaps or plant closer! A one-year-old gooseberry bush may look tiny, but it will soon grow to 1m wide and planting around it while young could hamper its growth.
- **Underplanting:** Growing under trees and shrubs has generally been discouraged in the past, but planting in vertical layers by height is key to plant communities. Throughout this book, I've given tips on which plants are suitable to being underplanted, by what and how.

Helping nature with gardens to forage

The best way to create a forage garden is to understand wild plant communities, and replicate the way they grow naturally. Plant communities can and do consist of only annual plants, but perennials provide a long-lived framework for planning edible planting that will thrive for years. They can even outlive us!

As a forager I'm conscious that in today's world there are far more people with far less wild land in which to forage. This increased density of people foraging in wild areas places more pressure on natural ecosystems.

Overharvesting plants or fungi can interrupt reproductive cycles. For instance, if every oyster mushroom is picked in an isolated colony, all the reproductive spore-producing parts that could have produced a new colony nearby are gone for a year. If the original colony then dies for whatever reason, we've had a negative impact on the ecosystem.

One solution to this problem is to ask governments to restore areas of lost wild land, thus increasing the

global area of natural ecosystems for people to forage once more. Many conservation charities are already doing this, which we can support through donations and memberships. The second critical solution is to help farmers switch back from intensive industrial farming practices to nature-led ones. This would increase forageable food on the fringes of farmland: in the hedgerows, paths and verges. This could have a significant impact, as farmland today makes up the largest proportion of accessible land on Earth.

A third solution that everyone can adopt today is to make gardens places for growing forageable food. By adding a handful of edible perennials or planning an entire garden full of them, we can grow plants and fungi to forage whenever we like. We can wander outdoors to pick crops as and when they are ready, in addition to, or instead of, relying solely on intensive traditional veg plots and wild foraging. Every food plant we grow ourselves takes pressure off the global food supply and, in turn, nature.

Above A new edible perennial plant community on our allotment shortly after planting, with mesh protection from deer and pheasants while plants establish. See it growing overleaf.

Regenerative growing and permaculture

Regenerative growing, or regenerative farming, restores the health of soil and ecosystems while also producing food. This goes beyond sustainable growing when it comes to overworked or damaged land because sustainable generally means to maintain, whereas regenerative means to improve.

To achieve regeneration while producing food, we must work with nature rather than against it. We need to use methods that look at a garden or farm holistically, considering its various ecosystems and soil together rather than as separate components; reducing or using no artificial inputs such as fertiliser and instead relying on natural organic matter; and, most important of all, using no pesticides since every spray can harm an ecosystem's delicate balance.

A key aspect of regenerative growing is permanence, described as permaculture, or permanent agriculture. Perennial edibles lie at the core of permaculture, providing a stable structure of plants that live from year-to-year and contribute to the living roots in soil year-round, which adds to the organic mass that feeds soil life. Healthy soil is fertile and alive with organisms that break down organic matter, making nutrients available for plant growth. By acting as a natural sponge around mineral particles in soil, this organic matter is also good for soil structure and water retention.

The big advantage of a regenerative permaculture approach, of seeing food crops as part of a natural ecosystem, is that the plant community becomes more self-sufficient, just as plants are in the wild, where cycles of plant growth and falling plant material (for example, leaves) keep soil fertile and alive to power plants in subsequent years. Exactly how I wanted the potato to grow in my parents' aspidistra!

This approach to growing food has long been proven to work, both by Indigenous communities around the world and by thousands of growers today. As a core component of these systems, perennial edibles help us to grow crops while increasing biodiversity, rather than harming it.

Edible plant communities

Plant communities are when plants grow alongside each other in balanced competition in the same area from year-to-year. A roadside verge with grasses and wildflowers is a plant community on a small scale, while a woodland is a plant community on a large scale.

Perennial edibles can be grown in traditional, well-spaced rows for intensive production. However, I'm interested in plant community design that is inspired by the wild habitats in which we forage, where plants are jumbled together rather than organised in the dedicated

Left Dense edible plant community a few months after planting, including chamomile, daylily (leaves), Welsh onions, Korean celery, oregano (purple flowers), wild rocket (yellow flowers), edible *Achillea ptarmica* and ox-eye daisy.

beds or row breaks favoured by a monoculture system. In communities, plants can grow densely, with multiple crops in the same area at different heights or with different ripening times through the year.

Stable plant communities grow in relative equilibrium, while others are dynamic, changing as plants spread or reacting to changes in weather, climate, disease, grazing and damage. Most wild plant communities are stable year-to-year but constantly dynamic, slowly changing over a longer period of time.

While monocultures are faster for sowing and harvesting crops in rows, they are unnaturally dense groups of one plant over a large area. Monocultures are also fragile and more vulnerable to disease and insect damage because these can spread quickly from plant to plant. Randomised plant communities are more resilient because individual plant species are grown in fewer numbers among many other species, thus slowing the spread of problem insects and disease. For instance, a monoculture field of kale is the jackpot for large and small white butterflies (*Pieris brassicae* and *Pieris rapae*), but grown among many other plants, the kale is more hidden.

Forest gardens are the best-known example of edible plant communities, mimicking vertical forest layers of trees, shrubs, climbers, large perennials, small, ground-covering plants, and subterranean root crops. They use plants such as fruit and nut trees, shade-tolerant fruit bushes and edible leaf crops. Such gardens produce food for us in different seasons and at different heights, which maximises the yield of every square metre.

There are many other habitats in the wild beyond forest gardens, however, as well as crops that can't grow in forest conditions. In this case, we can look to other habitats for inspiration to broaden the idea of edible plant communities beyond forest gardens, introducing a wider range of crops to the concept.

Types of habitat

In temperate regions the landscape is a patchwork of habitats, with grassland, wetland, scrub, woodland and larger forests adjoining and blending with each other. Hold this patchwork of habitats in mind when establishing perennial plant communities in your garden. You may decide on, or only have room for, one habitat type, or you might include two or more for variety.

WILD HABITATS	PLANT HEIGHT	SUITABLE FOR
Low grasslands, moorlands, sand dunes, alpine, scree, shallow soils (restricting growth), exposed and low-rainfall regions	Knee height or lower	Shorter edibles that need, and are happy growing in, lots of direct sunlight.
Taller grasslands, verges, wetlands, tall perennial communities and woodland edges	Waist to chest height	Larger edibles that still require lots of direct sunlight.
Scrubland, hedges, woodland edges	Head height (or just above)	Large edible shrubs and small trees tolerant of full sun with an understorey of smaller, shade-loving plants. Allow reasonable light through to the understorey.
Deciduous, evergreen or mixed woodlands and forests	Well over head height	Very large trees tolerant of full sun with multiple layers of small, shade-tolerant trees, shrubs, climbers, herbaceous perennials, annuals and biennials. Lower layers depend on the types of trees and light levels they let through.

Combine crops for easy harvest

Harvesting is one of the most time-consuming aspects of growing crops and an edible plant community risks making it harder to find ripe crops grown in a jumbled mix. This is particularly problematic when the main gardener who planned all the planting is helped by others who may not know where or what everything is, such as in a market or community garden. A solution I've created is to establish plant communities by crop type. This makes it easier to gather crops for meals or to sell. The Food Category Table shown here looks at this approach in more detail.

FOOD CATEGORY	CONDITIONS	EXAMPLE CROPS
Salad crops	Many perennial salad plants are small, need direct sunlight, and grow well with one another.	Stonecrop (*Hylotelephium*, formerly *Sedum*), *Viola*, daylily (*Hemerocallis*), red orache (*Atriplex hortensis* var. *rubra*), Good King Henry, scorzonera.
Sun-loving herbs	Many sun-loving herbs and spices need free-draining conditions and grow between knee and chest height, so it makes sense to cultivate these flavour boosters together.	Rosemary, sage, lavender, chives, bay (if clipped).
Cooked leafy greens	Often waist- to chest-high plants that grow best in full sun.	Perennial kale, Korean aster, coastal hog fennel, lovage.
Bulky greens	Waist- to head-high and grow best in full sun.	Broccauli, artichoke, Korean celery.
Fruit and nuts	Fruit and nuts grow well together, especially smaller hazelnuts which are similar in height to fruit trees.	Raspberry, blackcurrant, redcurrant and gooseberry are tolerant of the partial or dappled shade around smaller trees.
Shade-tolerant herbs	Knee- to waist-high herbs that tolerate shade and can be grown under trees and shrubs, or among smaller dense plant communities too.	Mint and sweet cicely.
Asparagus	Grows in dense competition in the wild and gardens, but for a high yield, grow asparagus in its own bed with less competition for light. Use a low ground cover such as strawberries or nasturtiums to prevent weeds.	
Root crops	As they are dug up when harvesting, it's better not to grow root crops in a complex plant community; otherwise you risk harming the roots of other plants.	Sunchoke, Chinese artichoke, dahlia.
Lime trees	Lime trees want to be enormous! They truly are forest trees, but can be kept small through coppicing, cutting the trunk to the ground – or pollarding (cut higher to 1.5–2m) – while the tree is dormant in winter.	Pruning allows you to grow lime trees among or near much smaller salad crops.

Right Globe artichoke 'Violet de Provence' among clouds of *Sanguisorba officinalis* 'Cangshan Cranberry'.

Opposite Evergreen crops gathered in winter from a small plant community; Welsh onion leaves, sage, thyme, rosemary and sweet cicely (with perennial kale in the background).

Ornamental edibles

Enjoyable, comfortable garden spaces are important for our mental health (we matter too!) and beautiful perennial edibles help food to fit right in. Almost every garden I've designed has perennial edibles in varying numbers among other plants, not only because they are edible but also because they are very beautiful and good for wildlife.

Apples, pears, plums and cherries have wonderful spring blossom and colourful autumn fruits. Herbs have glorious flowers and gorgeous leaves that are usually evergreen. The Szechuan strawberry (*Cornus kousa*) and the climber *Akebia longeracemosa* are grown for their flowers but also produce edible fruit. Architectural artichokes are outstanding border plants, as are fluffy asparagus leaves. *Hylotelephium* (formerly in the *Sedum* genus), daylilies (*Hemerocallis*) and *Viola* are grown in flower gardens but can also provide flowers and leaves to make excellent salads.

Dot one or two edible perennials throughout your garden or, with careful planning, create a beautiful garden that's entirely edible. A healthy version of Willy Wonka's chocolate factory.

Layers and succession

Successional planting, when a finished crop is replaced with a new one, is important in food growing to maximise yields. For decades, serious growers have planned to grow one crop such as potatoes and, once they've been harvested, plant another crop like radish or brassicas in the same spot. This produces two or three crops in the same space over one season.

Growing edibles in a plant community allows us to grow plants in layers with less effort. This involves planting in vertical layers, with trees growing above shrubs and ground-cover plants, but also in layers of time, where, for example, a ground-cover plant such as wild garlic crops in spring and grows in the same soil beneath a gooseberry bush that crops in summer. I think of this as a giant, changing 3D puzzle, with each plant a connecting piece.

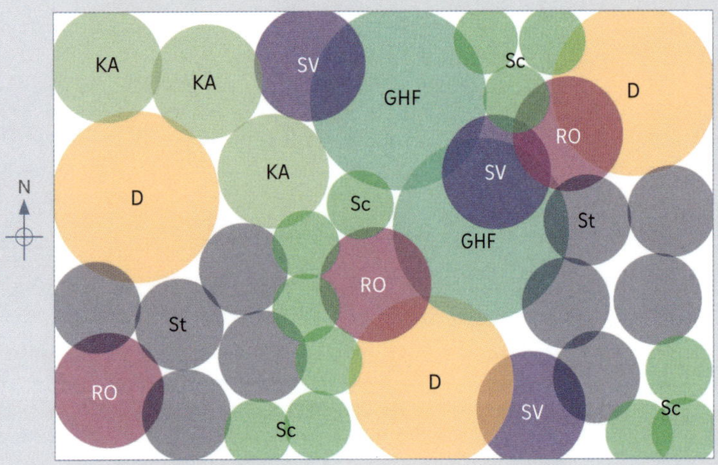

1 Perennial salad plant community

Knee-high or less. Full sun. Could be grown next to a lime tree coppiced or pollarded regularly to restrict growth and not shade the rest of the bed.

D Daylily (*Hemerocallis*)
GHF Giant hog fennel (*Peucedanum verticillare*)
KA Korean aster (*Doellingeria scabra*)
RO Red orache (*Atriplex hortensis*)
Sc Scorzonera (*Reichardia picroides*)
St Stonecrop (*Hylotelephium*)
SV Sweet violet (*Viola odorata*)

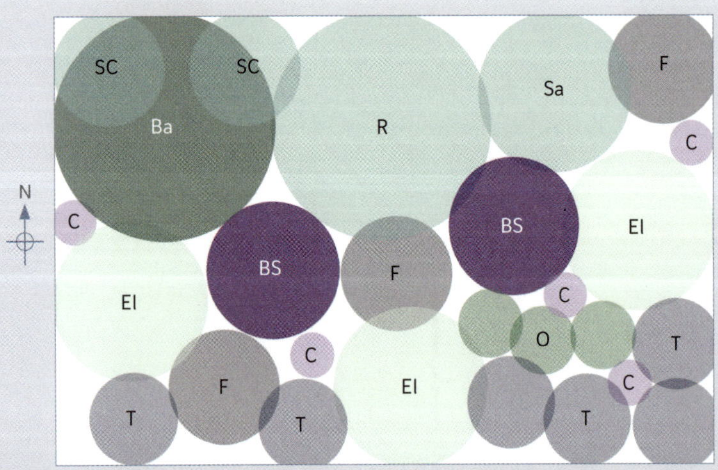

2 Herb plant community

Waist-high or less. Full sun. Some small, shade-tolerant plants can be grown behind the sun-loving ones if desired.

Ba Bay (*Laurus nobilis*)
BS Blackcurrant sage 'Nachtvlinder' (*Salvia microphylla*)
C Chives (*Allium schoenoprasum*)
EL English lavender (*Lavandula × angustifolia*)
F Fennel (*Foeniculum vulgare*)
O Oregano (*Origanum vulgare*)
R Rosemary (*Salvia rosmarinus*)
Sa Sage (*Salvia officinalis*)
SC Sweet cicely (*Myrrhis odorata*)
T Thyme 'English Winter' (*Thymus vulgaris*)

An edible plant community has the same sequential nature of one crop after the other, but it is less work because we are not sowing, growing, planting and clearing on repeat. The plants are already there each year, with no soil disturbance. With the right planning it's possible to grow a variety of perennial edibles in the same area for a succession of crops through the year.

Below Here are four different edible plant communities for 3m × 2m areas demonstrating it's possible to grow perennial crops in relatively small spaces. They are snapshots from real plant communities in our garden at home.

3 Cooked greens plant community

Waist- to head-high large plants. Full sun.

A layer of smaller, shade-tolerant edibles can be grown beneath these if desired. Lower sun lovers could be planted at the very front.

CA Chinese artichoke (*Stachys affinis*)
GA Globe artichoke (*Cynara cardunculus*)
O Oregano (*Origanum vulgare*)
PK Perennial kale (*Brassica oleracea* var. *ramosa*)
SV Sweet violet (*Viola odorata*)

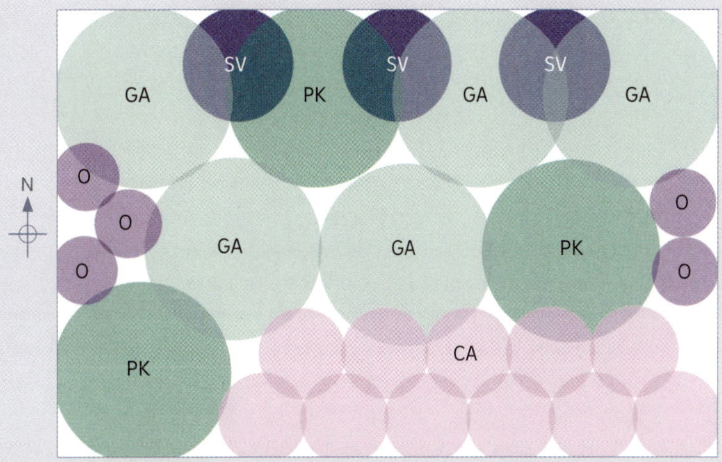

4 Fruit and nut plant community

At least head-high. Full sun and shade.

A multi-layered perennial edible community with a canopy layer of fruit and nut trees, followed by partially shade-tolerant fruit shrubs and then an understorey of shade- and partially shade-tolerant ground-cover plants.

G Gooseberry 'Leveller' (*Ribes uva-crispa*)
H Hazelnut 'Cosford Cob' (*Corylus avellana*)
Ra Raspberry 'Joan J' (*Rubus idaeus*)
Re Redcurrant (*Ribes rubrum*)
Rh Rhubarb 'Champagne' (*Rheum × hybridum*)
SC Sweet cicely (*Myrrhis odorata*)
SH Siebold's hosta (*Hosta sieboldiana*)
St Strawberry 'Cambridge Favourite' (*Fragaria × ananassa*)

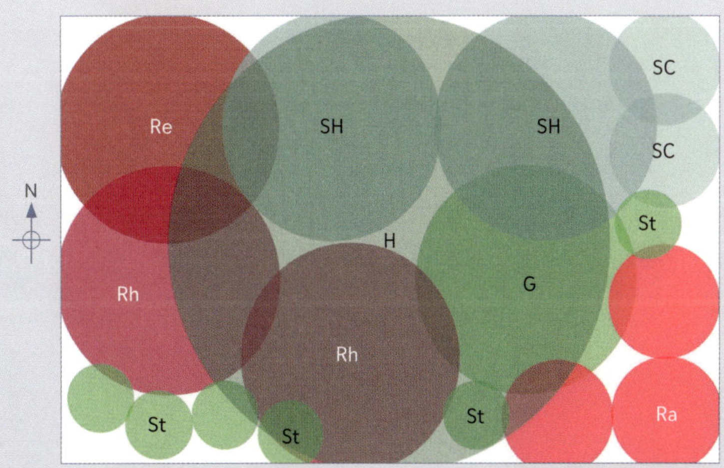

Livestock and plant communities

It's possible to grow an edible plant community in the same space as animals – animals are part of wild ecosystems after all. It just needs a bit of thought about the heights of the plants and the right density of animals for the area.

Two of our edible plant communities are in the same area as our chickens; I simply selected plants I knew would grow large enough, so their leaves were above pecking height, or that they don't like. Chickens tend to eat succulent leafy greens, such as dandelion and dock, from head height down, so tall perennial kale, artichokes, fruit bushes and fruit trees grow over our chickens. Spreading ground covers that are resilient or off-putting to their scratching for worms or dust baths work too – try sweet violet (*Viola odorata*) and oregano (*Origanum vulgare*). New plantings need protecting with wire mesh to keep the chickens out until they've grown to the right size.

Sheep, cows and even deer can be part of an edible plant community with the right planning. These herbivores are useful for eating grasses underneath fruit and nut trees, helping maintain the right balance for wildflowers. They may eat leaves from lower branches, but they can't reach all of a large tree. Wild deer roam our farm and I've found nettles help protect the shoots of our coppiced hazel trees, and they don't like spiky blackberries. They don't touch scented herbs at all or hairy leaves.

Self-seeding annual crops

It's worth including a shout-out to some annual food plants that we can treat like perennials because they self-seed and grow freely by themselves each year. My favourites (shown opposite) include:

1. **Borage (*Borago officinalis*):** Beautiful, blue flowers or white on the cultivar 'Alba'. Flowers and leaves are edible and can be used in salads and as a garnish. Leaves are hairy, so the soft young leaves are best.
2. **Chamomile (*Matricaria recutita*):** The sweet species used for chamomile tea – beware others which can taste like rubber tyres! Narrow leaves are edible and can be used in salads, with the flowers mainly used fresh or dried for a calming tea.
3. **Cornflower (*Centaurea cyanus*):** Edible petals for salad or garnish. Cultivars available in shades of blue, white, pink and, my favourite, black-purple 'Blackball'.
4. **Nasturtium (*Tropaeolum majus*):** Peppery salad leaves and flowers, plus the fresh seeds can be pickled like capers. 'Alaska' is compact with beautiful, variegated leaves.
5. **Pot marigold (*Calendula officinalis*):** Tasty edible petals, which are a little peppery and easy to pick to sprinkle in salad or use as a garnish. The flowers of 'Sherbet Fizz' and 'Touch of Red Buff' have pale orange petals with tawny undersides. 'Snow Princess' has cream flowers.
6. **Red orache (*Atriplex hortensis* var. *rubra*):** Beautiful, purple-red leaves that are tasty as salad when young and can be used like spinach when older. A good bulk salad leaf.

Left I love the beautiful wild roe deer that roam our garden, and while I exclude them from some crops, I've planned large edible plant communities that include them.

1

2

3

4

5

6

Save your own seeds

Collect seeds from plants by keeping an eye on their flowers as they die back. Seeds or seed-pods will follow and when they come away freely from the plant, or the pods begin to split open, the seeds are ready to collect. Gently tap the seeds into a paper envelope held underneath, labelling immediately with the plant name, date and location collected because it's easy to forget what they are or muddle them up. You can either sow where you'd like them straight away, replicating nature, or store in a cool, dark and dry place until ready to use.

Right Fennel seeds fall away easily when ripe and can be collected in a paper packet or envelope.

Experimentation in face of climate change and extreme weather

Human-accelerated climate change is upon us and according to the Met Office and other trusted meteorological sources, it will now quickly get worse. Unless global leaders rapidly get their acts together, between now and 2100 we are going to see extreme changes in climate and weather patterns. This presents real challenges for food growers at the forefront of climate impacts. My best advice now is to make experimentation a key part of your growing plans.

Test plant hardiness yourself

As the climate changes it's important we all learn to experiment with crops in order to test their tolerances in different parts of the world. It is useful to try this in different microclimates too, because plants that ordinarily wouldn't survive in a cold region just might in a sheltered garden or urban area.

In our old city garden, along with others I've designed, I have been able to grow perennials that had previously been reported as unable to survive British temperatures. Pineapple guava (*Feijoa sellowiana*), common olive (*Olea europaea*) and avocado (*Persea americana*) not only survived but fruited. On the flip side, plants like lettuce struggled in the drier, hotter summers. This shift in climate is happening rapidly across the world and planting zones will shift with it. In Part Two, I've included hardiness zones and the minimum temperature range a plant can endure. You can use horticultural fleece to protect some plants to get them through frosty periods. You can also put potted plants in a cold frame or bring them inside during spells of frost.

Using this book

The next section of this book contains my favourite easy to grow and high yielding perennial crops, grouped into vegetables, fruits, herbs, nuts, flowers and fungi. Each plant profile begins with a rating for effort, scored from 0 (no effort) to 5 (significant work) and tastiness. You'll also find detailed information on nutrition (see below for more on this) and practical growing advice. While these profiles focus on my personal favourites, each chapter ends with a short list of additional plants that are also worth considering. The interview section following the plant profiles share inspiring examples from across the world of perennial growers, foragers and scientists.

Nutrition

The nutrition section for each species profile provides an overview of known notable components, with rankings high to low based on Recommended Daily Allowance (RDA) and by comparable crops. For some of the more unusual crops, there is limited data available at the moment and I have instead shared what is known about them or the nutrition of closely related crops where they are likely to be similar.

Plan for flexible harvests

We also need to adjust our expectations. There may be some years when crops are poor due to excessive rain or drought. In normal years our fruit trees are laden with apples, pears and stone fruits. But climate change is making spring begin earlier, which means that trees blossom earlier as well. This early blossom is more likely to be hit by late frosts killing the flowers, preventing pollination and giving us years without any tree fruit at all.

If some perennial crops deliver in 8 out of 10 years, that's still good. Other perennial crops may only deliver in 2 out of 10 years, but that is still useful; it's still food. If we are growing crops like avocados, bananas or peaches at the edge of their hardiness limits, where they can survive but not normally fruit, that's okay, because in hotter years they may well provide a bountiful harvest.

Don't give up

If a plant or crop fails in one year, keep trying. Plants and ecosystems are complex living entities, and it is not always possible to identify what caused a crop to fail. The reason may be different to what you expect, making it important to try multiple times across different years if it doesn't work at first – especially as the climate is already making weather unpredictable.

Below Perennial edibles are easy and cheap to start from seed or cuttings. These seedlings may be small now, but they will grow to fill an entire garden at little expense.

Vegetables

Imagine a world where vegetables grow in your garden every year without the hassle of ground preparation and sowing seeds. That is the promise of perennial edibles and I'm happy to say, after years of research, that I've discovered a good number of easy perennial vegetables I can recommend, which cover multiple food and nutrient types – from leaves eaten raw in salads to bulky cooked vegetables that fill you up, all packed with healthy nutrition, such as vitamin C, calcium, iron and carbs. Importantly, I've grown and taste tested everything, whittling my list down to only the easy and delicious plants I'd feel confident serving friends and family. Many foraged perennial vegetables taste bitter, and we'd only eat them if nothing else was available. Instead, let's focus on flavour!

Below Globe artichokes (blue pots, first two rows) are easy to grow from seed in spring and cost very little to get started. Padron peppers (blue pots, third row) won't survive freezing temperatures, but they'll live for years if you bring them indoors over winter.

ASPARAGUS

EFFORT 3/5
TASTINESS 5/5

Asparagus officinalis

Given how expensive asparagus is, yet how productive a small patch can be, it's well worth growing this spring treat.

NUTRITION:
Potassium (moderate)
Calcium (low)
Phosphorus (low-moderate)
Magnesium (low-moderate)
Manganese (low-moderate)
Copper (moderate)
Iron (moderate, especially raw)
Vitamin B1/thiamine (moderate)
Vitamin B9/folate (high)
Vitamin K (high)

FAMILY: Asparagaceae
MAX SIZE: 100cm tall, 40cm wide
PLANT: spring
HARVEST: spring, early summer
POT-FRIENDLY: no
SOIL: free-draining, nutrient-rich
SITUATION: full sun
HARDINESS: H4 (-10°C to -5°C)
ORIGIN: mainland Europe to Mongolia and northern Russia

Raw asparagus snaps so easily because each stem is loaded with moisture, making it brittle. When first picked, the cut drips with the water that makes asparagus so sweet and tasty. The sooner you eat it, the better it tastes, which means few asparagus plants ever leave our veg plot.

Grow

Wild asparagus can be a vigorous plant – I've seen it growing out of sand dunes and pebble beaches, or through grassland. In gardens asparagus seems weaker and, while I love growing a mix of purple and green cultivars, 10 years down the line I have to admit that purple asparagus simply doesn't have enough oomph for me. 'Purple Pacific' and 'Burgundine' both look and taste wonderful, but are noticeably weaker and prone to dwindling away. Reliable cultivars for me include green 'Backlim' and 'Guelph Millennium', the latter being reportedly slightly hardier, and that certainly bears out for me.

Asparagus plants come as bareroot crowns that look like alien tarantulas. Plant the crowns 45cm apart and 20cm deep, with a small 10cm mound in the middle to support the centre of the crown. Cover with soil and keep the bed clear of other plants, topping with 3–5cm of compost each autumn. You can also buy plants in pots, which I've found take just as well, or grow asparagus from seed, which is cheaper and easier than it sounds: just sow in 7cm pots of compost in spring.

Left Once established asparagus plants will supply succulent spears each spring for decades.

Opposite Underplant asparagus with nasturtium between rows for a weed-suppressing groundcover.

Asparagus beetle grubs produce a foam to lurk in while they nibble leaves, thus weakening the plants. Pick off adults in spring to reduce their number.

Don't pick any spears for the first two years while the asparagus settles in – a painful wait but worth it because asparagus will crop for at least 20 years. Support the fluffy foliage with sticks at the ends of each row and twine on either side of the plants.

Gather

As shoots emerge in late spring to early summer, use a sharp knife to cut spears at soil level. Do this carefully, so as not to damage the new shoots below ground. It's easy to know when to harvest asparagus and when to stop for the rest of the year by picking only thick spears. As soon as they look noticeably thinner, about a pencil thin, stop picking and let the plant grow and build up energy for next year. Picking shoots will encourage multiple new shoots to grow from the crown, ultimately strengthening the plants.

Eat

I don't need to tell you how delicious asparagus can be. Steaming, searing or even lightly boiling can help bring out the unique flavour in different ways. Personally, I favour searing in a hot pan, though I do have a thing for that slightly boiled flavour, which reminds me of the 1980s.

AVOCADO

EFFORT
TASTINESS

Persea americana and *Persea americana* var. *drymifolia*

Avocado trees can be slightly hardier than people realise, and they grow happily all over cities and towns across warmer southern regions of the temperate world. Urban micro-climates created by the shelter of buildings, as well as global warming, has enabled them to survive where they couldn't before.

NUTRITION:
Monounsaturated fats (high)
Fibre (moderate)
Potassium (moderate)
Copper (high)
Magnesium (moderate)
Vitamin B3/niacin equivalent (moderate)
Vitamin B5/pantothenic acid (high)
Vitamin B6/pyridoxine (moderate)
Vitamin B9/folate (low-moderate)
Vitamin E (moderate)

FAMILY: Lauraceae
MAX SIZE: 4.5–7m tall, 3.5–7m wide
PLANT: spring, summer
HARVEST: mid-summer
POT-FRIENDLY: no
SOIL: any free-draining
SITUATION: full sun
HARDINESS: varies with cultivar (see below)
ORIGIN: South America and southern USA

We eat avocado as a vegetable but by definition it's a fruit formed from the plant's ovary. Avocado ovaries contain one ovule, which becomes the large seed when fertilised. It is the main fruit of note within the laurel family, and a distant relative of the bay tree (see page 102).

The photo on the opposite page is a close-up of a fruiting tree towering over a small garden in central London, England. As the climate changes, it is worth testing the hardiness of these perennial crops, focusing on hardier cultivars.

Grow

Plant an avocado as you would any tree, providing lots of space. Some avocados such as 'Hass' are big trees, growing upward of 7m or more and almost as wide. Other cultivars, such as 'Mexicola Grande' and 'Bacon', are smaller at around 4.5m.

While 'Hass' is widely sold in shops, it's the cultivars bred from *Persea americana* var. *drymifolia* that are hardier, reportedly withstanding short periods of -9°C once mature. These include 'Mexicola Grande' and 'Bacon', which are currently hard to obtain outside the USA, though their fruit – and the seed within – occasionally appear in European shops.

Avocado flowers open for two days, their reproductive parts alternating gender between days. In some cultivars the flowers open with the

female pistil active on the first day before closing and transitioning to the male stamens activating the next day. This is known as protogynous dichogamy, while the reverse order, male first and then female, is protandrous dichogamy.

When avocado flowers open as female first, they're known as Type A, and this group includes the cultivars 'Hass' and 'Mexicola Grande'. Type B are male first and include 'Bacon', 'Fuerte' and 'Zutano'. It's a myth you need an A and B type to pollinate each other; avocados are self-pollinating. However, both types next to each other will marginally aid pollination.

Grow avocados from seed by putting in a plastic bag containing a little damp compost, then seal and place in a warm, dark cupboard. Check regularly to see if the seed has split and a root is emerging. As soon as you spot this, plant into a 2-litre pot of compost with the tip of the seed just above the surface.

Gather

Avocados lift from the tree easily when fully grown. They ripen best after picking; give a gentle squeeze to check ripeness. In colder climates, such as mid- to north Europe, a normal summer may not be long enough to ripen the fruit, which will instead ripen in autumn or winter. You can pick unripe fruit to ripen on a warm, sunny windowsill.

Eat

Avocados are well known for their use in guacamole or as a salad ingredient. They are nutritionally dense and good for heart health, thanks to potassium and good monounsaturated fats. They are very low in sugar and have zero cholesterol.

Right 'Hass' avocados ripening in a sheltered London microclimate.

Opposite Hardy avocado 'Mexicola Grande' is easy to grow from seed on a windowsill.

BROCCAULI

EFFORT 3/5
TASTINESS 5/5

Brassica oleracea 'Nine Star Perennial'

'Nine Star' is a perennial cultivar of *Brassica* and grows white florets reminiscent of a cauliflower, which, to me, taste like a cross between a cauliflower and broccoli spears. Taste it to see what you think. I've given this cultivar the combined name, broccauli! Whatever it's called, broccauli is delicious steamed. A useful bulky perennial veg to add to our list.

NUTRITION:
(based on annual tenderstem broccoli):
Fibre (high)
Protein (moderate)
Potassium (moderate)
Calcium (moderate)
Iron (moderate)
Vitamin A (moderate)
Vitamin B1/thiamine (moderate)
Vitamin B5/pantothenic acid (moderate)
Vitamin B6/pyridoxine (moderate)
Vitamin B9/folate (high)
Vitamin C (high)
Vitamin E (moderate)
Phytonutrients (high)

FAMILY: Brassicaceae
MAX SIZE: 1m tall, 1m wide
GROW: spring
HARVEST: spring
POT-FRIENDLY: yes, large pots 40cm-plus
SOIL: any free-draining
SITUATION: full sun
HARDINESS: H5 (-15°C to -10°C)
ORIGIN: Britain, France and Spain

Above Broccauli can be a short-lived perennial, thankfully it's super easy to grow from cuttings.

Opposite You can eat the leaves of broccauli in the same way as its close relative kale.

Grow

'Nine Star' is bought or shared as cuttings because these are genetic clones of the parent plant, and grow in the same way. Seed-grown plants can vary compared to their parents, with the chance of something better or the risk of something worse. If you're interested in plant breeding, it's worth giving this a whirl, but for those of us wanting to grow 'Nine Star', it's best to stick to cuttings.

Take cuttings of side shoots that are about 15cm long, cutting just beneath a leaf node (the point where a leaf grows). Remove the lower two-thirds of leaves and gently push that part of the stem into a pot of compost, three to five cuttings per 9cm pot. Water a little, cover with a transparent lid or sealable plastic bag to hold in humidity, and place somewhere warm and bright but not in direct sunlight, such as a north-facing windowsill. Within a few weeks cuttings should root, evidenced by new leaf growth.

Being hardy, 'Nine Star' can be planted outside at any time of year, but it's best to wait for the warmer months when plants will grow quickly. Leave at least an 80cm space between plants. As they grow, plants may need to be supported in windy spots.

Be sure to pick all florets and keep snipping off any other stray flower-buds to prevent seeding. This can help maintain strong growth from year-to-year, though it's best to be prepared for plants to slow down after a few years. When this happens, replace with new cuttings.

In summer, plants may need to be covered with a fine insect mesh to prevent large and small white butterflies (*Pieris brassicae* and *Pieris rapae*) laying eggs, as their caterpillars devour brassica leaves.

Gather

In spring, 'Nine Star' will produce many florets that turn a cream colour, though they are edible at any stage. Cut off with sharp secateurs or a knife at about 20cm long, which should still be succulent rather than tough. Like tenderstem broccoli, 'Nine Star' can keep growing new shoots over a number of weeks for successive crops.

Eat

'Nine Star' can be eaten raw as a snack or in salads. It's perhaps better suited to cooking, which I find helps the flavour. Steam, boil or fry as you would tenderstem broccoli. Broccoli stems are one of the more nutritionally dense vegetables we can eat, making it a good idea to add them regularly to meals.

CARDOON

EFFORT
TASTINESS

Cynara cardunculus

Eaten in Italy and other Mediterranean countries where they evolved, cardoons are the spikier ornamental parent to the globe artichoke (see page 44), which is smaller in stature. Unlike artichokes, we eat the inner part of cardoon leaf stems. It is also possible to eat the inner part of the buds and flower stems in the same way as artichokes if picked young and tender like baby artichokes.

NUTRITION:
Carbohydrates (moderate)
Fibre (moderate)
Potassium (high)
Calcium (moderate)
Magnesium (moderate)
Polyphenols – phenolic acids (high), flavonoids (moderate)

FAMILY: Asteraceae
MAX SIZE: 2.5m tall, 1m wide
GROW: spring
HARVEST: mid-summer
POT-FRIENDLY: no
SOIL: any free-draining
SITUATION: full sun
HARDINESS: H5 (-15°C to -10°C)
ORIGIN: southern Europe and northern Africa

Grow

Cardoons are very easy to grow and keep going for years. They need full sunlight, soil that doesn't get too wet in winter, and some shelter from the coldest frosts. Otherwise, they are vigorous and hardier than globe artichokes, requiring little attention. Very large perennials that tower well over head height, cardoons need at least 1m of space per plant, sometimes slightly more.

Grow cardoons easily from seed, sowing one seed 1cm deep into 10cm pots of compost in spring. Grow inside initially to protect from frost, then, when all risk of frost is over and the seedlings have at least

Left After peeling cardoon stems, soak in a bowl of lemon juice until cooking to prevent oxidation turning them brown.

Opposite Cardoons are large and architecturally beautiful plants worth a place in any sunny part of the garden.

four true leaves, either plant into a bigger 3-litre pot outside or into their final spot. In summer warmth, they will grow rapidly.

You can also gently tease off the side shoots from the base of established plants in spring using a trowel, making sure each shoot has some roots to grow. Pot into compost as per seedlings.

Gather

Although cardoon leaf stalks can be picked and eaten as they are, you can reduce the bitterness by excluding sunlight for four to six weeks (this technique is called blanching). Traditionally, near the Mediterranean, this is done by mounding earth up around the leaves when plants are 1m tall. In wetter climates, this can lead to leaf rot, and so it's better and less messy to wrap the stems in breathable hessian coffee or potato sacks, tying with natural twine. Double-wrap to properly exclude light.

Once ready to harvest, snap leaf stalks off by hand by twisting to the side, as you would for rhubarb (see page 96). Choose leaves that look full grown and healthy with large stalks.

Eat

The edible part of cardoons is the inner section of the midrib of the leaf. Cut the leafy part off, leaving only the stem, then use a potato peeler to peel away the back and a knife for any tough bits.

Chop horizontally into 2–3cm chunks – this cuts any stringy bits – and place in a large bowl of acidulated water, which means water with a good squeeze of lemon juice. Acid from the lemon will stop the cardoon turning brown through oxidation.

Cardoon is edible raw but can taste less bitter when cooked. Roast for 45 minutes or boil for 15–20 minutes – either way, check if tender and cook for longer if not. Baby flower stems and buds are peeled and cooked in the same way as young artichoke buds (see page 45).

CHINESE ARTICHOKE

EFFORT 1/5
TASTINESS 4/5

Stachys affinis

Like a potato, Chinese artichoke is a root tuber, an underground organ that plants use to store energy. Nutrient-dense, Chinese artichokes are packed with useful food components, especially carbohydrates that give us energy, potassium, fibre and slightly more protein than potato or sweet potato.

NUTRITION:
Carbohydrate (high)
Fibre (high)
Protein (moderate)
Potassium (high)
Phosphorus (moderate)
Iron (moderate)
Calcium (moderate)
Magnesium (moderate)
Oligosaccharides (high)
Polyphenols (high)
Saponins (high)

FAMILY: Lamiaceae
MAX SIZE: 60cm tall, 50cm wide
HARVEST: winter
POT-FRIENDLY: yes
SOIL: any free-draining
SITUATION: full sun
HARDINESS: H7 (< -20°C)
ORIGIN: China to Myanmar

Above Harvested Chinese artichokes don't need peeling; once cleaned they can be eaten raw or cooked

Although small, Chinese artichokes are easy to grow and are delicious to eat. In the world of perennial edibles, bulky and filling crops are somewhat limited, making this odd-looking but tasty crop valuable.

Grow

In spring plant tubers of Chinese artichoke on their sides in a sunny spot, about 7cm deep and 45cm apart, in rows or a staggered grid. They'll soon grow into low-growing mounds of leaves, which can be picked, dried and used to make tea. Leave them to grow through the season, removing seedlings of other plants that might start growing between them.

Through the course of the year Chinese artichokes will form a number of new tubers below ground. The plants and tubers are very hardy and can be left over winter. Any tubers left in the ground after harvest will grow in the spring, producing a new batch of tubers. Repeat this process every year for a continuous perennial crop. Leave the flowers for pollinators – this won't affect tuber production.

Gather

Tubers will be ready to harvest from around early winter (around November in Europe). Use a garden fork to gently lever the plant and tubers out of the ground, shaking off as much soil as you can. Replant one tuber per plant to grow in spring. Rinse the knobbly tubers well under water to remove all remaining soil.

Eat

There's no need to peel Chinese artichokes, as the whole tuber is edible raw. To me, they taste and have a texture reminiscent of crunchy water chestnuts. You can pickle them raw, and many people turn them purple by adding some beetroot or red shisho.

I enjoy Chinese artichokes in stir-fries by boiling them in water for a minute first and then frying as part of the mix. They can be eaten like new potatoes by boiling for 15 minutes or steaming until soft. Eat them like that or fry them slightly after boiling to brown them.

Below Chinese artichokes are low-growing, herbaceous perennials that crop best in full sun.

COASTAL HOG FENNEL

EFFORT 1/5
TASTINESS 4/5

Peucedanum japonicum

It's the leaves I love most about coastal hog fennel, which are ever so slightly glaucous and smooth with luxuriously round leaflets on large compound leaves. I would include these plants in gardens for the pristine and unusual foliage alone. They look so delicious I could eat them and, thankfully, they're edible, so I do.

NUTRITION:
Polyphenols, including flavonoids (high)

Despite limited credible data elsewhere, it is considered to have moderate levels of potassium, phosphorus, iron, calcium, as well as vitamins A, C and K.

FAMILY: Apiaceae
MAX SIZE: 1m tall, 70cm wide
GROW: spring
HARVEST: spring, summer, autumn
POT-FRIENDLY: no
SOIL: any
SITUATION: full sun
HARDINESS: H7 (< -20°C)
ORIGIN: south-east China, Japan and Philippines

Grow

Sow seeds of coastal hog fennel in spring just below the surface of compost in seed trays or pots. Grow in a sunny protected area, such as a windowsill or unheated polytunnel or greenhouse, or outside a bit later in the season as the weather warms. Water gently and cover with a transparent lid.

Once the seedlings have two to four adult leaves, pot them into their own 10cm pots and grow on until they are larger with six or more adult leaves. Then plant them in their final positions, giving them about 70cm or so space in full sun.

The name coastal hog fennel comes from the plant's original habitats along the coasts of south-east China and around the islands of Japan south to the Philippines. Here the plants receive full sunlight, which they need to grow well in gardens, making them better suited to low plant communities (see page 20) rather than in the shade of forest gardens.

Really, coastal hog fennel is a biennial or triennial, growing leaves in the first and second years before flowering, setting seed and dying in its final year. For this reason, it's worth sowing seeds for the first two years to start a succession. Once established, the plants will self-seed naturally, allowing you to choose seedlings near the dead parent plant to grow in future. Or collect the seeds to grow yourself in spring.

Left Coastal hog fennel has large, slightly succulent leaves that are great as salad or lightly steamed.

Opposite Their leaves are evergreen making them a valuable crop that can be harvested in winter.

Gather

Pick leaves as you need to use them. The leaf stems are edible but tougher than the fleshy leaves, so I would just gather the leafy parts.

Eat

Discard the leaf stems. Tender leaves can be used in salad; they're fleshy with just enough bite. Flavour-wise, I would describe them as somewhere between mangetout, kale and parsley with an umami undercurrent. Fresh new leaves are particularly delicious raw. If you find flavours like this too much on their own, mix them with milder leaves of crops like scorzonera (see page 42).

Older leaves can still be used raw but are perhaps better steamed or boiled lightly for a minute to wilt them. They can also be fried. Their flavour works well in Asian cuisine.

COMMON BISTORT

EFFORT
TASTINESS

Bistorta officinalis

When we moved to Hebden Bridge in Yorkshire, we heard rumours of a dish called dock pudding. Then people started proudly telling us about the celebrity-judged dock pudding competition in the nearby village of Mytholmroyd, where people compete to cook the tastiest version of this local delicacy. It turns out the dish is neither a pudding nor made from dock. Instead, the recipe calls for the leaves of one of my favourite wildflowers, the common bistort, cooked with some pinhead oatmeal and onions. It is tastier than it sounds and nutritious – read on to learn more!

NUTRITION:
Manganese (high)
Iron (high)
Zinc (high)
Copper (moderate)
Calcium (moderate)
Vitamin C (moderate)
Polyphenols (high)

FAMILY: Polygonaceae
MAX SIZE: 70cm tall, 70cm wide
GROW: spring, summer
HARVEST: spring, summer
POT FRIENDLY: yes
SOIL: moisture-retentive
SITUATION: full sun
HARDINESS: H7 (< -20°C)
ORIGIN: temperate Eurasia and Morocco

Grow

Common bistort is a wildflower of damp meadows, which tells us everything we need to grow it. Thriving in damp, water-retentive soil in full sun, due to its evolution in competitive grasslands, it is a prime candidate for sunny edible perennial plant communities growing among other plants. Leaves emerge in early spring before the most beautiful, pale pink tufts of flowers, which look to me a little like floating marshmallows.

It is possible to grow from seed sown in spring on the surface of a seed tray of compost, watered with a fine rose watering can. Once germinated, with three leaves or so, carefully pot each seedling into individual 9cm pots to grow larger before planting outside. It's slightly easier and faster to buy some young plants to plant out in spring. Common bistort can be grown in 30–40cm pots, as long as they don't dry out.

Once established, the plants will naturally spread gently from underground horizontal roots that

Below It's the fresh spring leaves of common bistort that are eaten as a cooked green. It has a mild, spinach-like flavour.

Opposite Common bistort is a beautiful wildflower, shown here happily growing in dense competition in our damp meadow.

produce new shoots, called rhizomes. In your garden, you can dig up pieces of rhizome with leaves and roots to plant elsewhere – but don't do this from the wild, as digging up wild plants is illegal.

Gather

Pick the young leaves in spring and early summer. As with all plants in the wild or your garden, be sure not to take every leaf off, especially from young plants, as they need them to photosynthesise.

Eat

Use the leaves as you would spinach, either frying, steaming or boiling. To make the world-famous dock pudding, I spoke to born-and-bred Calderdale Yorkshireman, John Butterworth, who revealed his secret recipe:

'Pick a carrier-bag full of young leaves, with no stalks. Wash and chop, then place in a large saucepan in about 2cm of boiling water. When the leaves turn colour, cook for a couple of minutes more. Drain off most of the water, but keep it to one side. Fry a couple of onions, finely chopped, until golden. Stir into the cooked docks, then add a few handfuls of pinhead oatmeal and stir everything together. Add some of the retained water if it looks a bit dry (the oatmeal soaks up lots of water), and some salt and pepper to taste.'

For extra flavour, serve with chopped pieces of fried bacon, oyster mushroom or halloumi.

FRENCH SCORZONERA

EFFORT
TASTINESS

Reichardia picroides

Scorzonera, what an incredible edible perennial. While it may look superficially like a dandelion or one of the many thousands of dandelion-like species, in my opinion this is much tastier. The leaves have a similar texture and flavour to a sweet, non-bitter lettuce leaf. Anyone who's foraged edible leaves and adjusted to lemony or bitter tastes will understand why this is a joy.

NUTRITION: Despite limited credible data, it is known to have antioxidant properties.

FAMILY: Asteraceae
MAX SIZE: 30cm tall, 30cm wide
HARVEST: year round
POT-FRIENDLY: yes
SOIL: any
SITUATION: full sun to partial shade
HARDINESS: H4 (-10°C to -5°C)
ORIGIN: Mediterranean

Grow

Scorzonera can be grown easily from seed. They produce fluffy seed heads like a small dandelion clock. If you know someone who grows some, ask for a pinch of the seeds to grow, or they are available to buy. During spring and summer, sow the tiny seeds on the surface of damp compost in 7–9cm pots or a seed tray, spacing them out, or alternatively use modular seed trays.

Cover with a transparent lid to lock in humidity and place somewhere warm, such as a windowsill, polytunnel or greenhouse. Within a few weeks the seeds should germinate. Plant the seedlings into their own dedicated 10cm pots of compost when they have four to six leaves. Once the young plants fill the pot, they can be planted in their final position outside.

Plant in full sun to partial shade, 30cm apart, to give each plant space while growing close enough to block other plants from seeding in between them. This creates a dense edible ground cover, which is useful in sunnier areas of plant communities. For containers, grow one plant in a 20cm pot or three to five plants in larger pots.

Scorzonera appear not to be eaten by slugs and snails, which I think we can all agree is an absolute bonus.

Left It's the leaves of French scorzonera that are eaten as a salad leaf or cooked green.

Gather

Pick leaves by hand, as needed, like a cut-and-come-again lettuce. As with all plants, leave at least 30–50 per cent of the leaves on each plant, so they can create energy through photosynthesis. Leaves are available year round, though they grow fastest in the warmer months. Flowering makes no difference to leaf production or flavour.

Eat

Eat as you would lettuce. Makes an excellent non-bitter base to salads and sandwiches. Delicious with a drizzle of good olive oil. Can also be added to cooked meals like risotto, pasta and stir-fries; the leaves will wilt in the same way as rocket.

Above I bought one French scorzonera plant and then grew all of these for free from seed; it was easy.

Right French scorzonera looks superficially similar to wildflowers in the hawkbit and dandelion families.

GLOBE ARTICHOKE

EFFORT ●●○○○
TASTINESS ●●●●●

Cynara cardunculus Scolymus Group

Statuesque and striking, globe artichokes are the same species as cardoons (see page 34) and cultivated for their edible flower-buds. Although globe artichokes aren't the most nutritious plants in this book, their potassium and folate components are useful. Besides, they taste delicious, and it's the flavour I grow them for.

NUTRITION:
Potassium (moderate)
Calcium (low-moderate)
Vitamin B9/folate (moderate)
Polyphenols (moderate)

FAMILY: Asteraceae
MAX SIZE: 2m tall, 1m wide
HARVEST: mid-summer
POT-FRIENDLY: no
SOIL: any free-draining
SITUATION: full sun
HARDINESS: H5 (-15°C to -10°C)
ORIGIN: southern Europe and northern Africa

Grow

It's possible to grow globe artichoke as annuals, as they can germinate and flower in their first year – but we're more interested in their perennial nature. The only tricky part of growing globe artichokes is winter. In warmer, drier climates they'll sail through no problem, but in wetter or colder areas the crown can rot.

To help, try cutting back the stems in autumn and covering them with their dead leaves to form a cover, or use a mulch of straw. Importantly, choose the cultivar best suited to your garden's conditions. I'm growing 'Tavor', which is a marginally hardier cultivar. In areas with drier winter conditions, 'Green Globe' and purple-budded 'Violetta' are good options.

Allow a 1m space for each plant, as they are large perennials. As with cardoons, globe artichokes are easy to grow from seed in spring. Sow 1cm deep into 9cm pots of compost inside on a windowsill, or in a greenhouse or polytunnel, and grow until the plants have five to six leaves before planting into larger 3-litre pots or the ground outside when all risk of frost has passed.

Below This plant was grown from seed in spring and is cropping in summer of the same year, they are vigorous plants.

Gather

Harvest the flower-buds when they are either the size of golf balls for baby artichokes, or wait until they are much larger – just before they start to open – for full size. Use secateurs to cut through the tough stems. I prefer harvesting baby artichokes because there is less fiddling about when it comes to eating them.

Eat

Baby artichokes are prepared by chopping off the pointy tip of the bud and peeling away the toughest outer bracts to reveal the pale inner bracts (the green scales around the bud sometimes incorrectly called leaves). Use a potato peeler or sharp knife to peel the hard outer part of the stem; the inner part can be eaten. Slice in half vertically. Fry, steam or boil for 15 minutes or so until completely tender. The baby artichokes can then be eaten or allowed to cool and stored in a jar of oil for use in salads or on pizza.

Prepare full-sized globe artichokes by cutting the top quarter off horizontally and removing the hard stem. Steam the entire flower-bud for roughly 25 minutes until the scales lift away easily by hand, a good sign they are cooked. Alternatively, cover in about a tablespoon of oil, seal tightly with foil to lock in moisture, and roast for 1 hour 15 minutes at 200°C (fan oven) – make sure the foil has no gaps, otherwise the globe artichokes can dry out. Once cooked, remove the hairy inner bit called the choke, or you will choke. It comes out easily once cooked.

Eat the flesh on the scales by scraping with your teeth: there isn't a lot, but it is tasty. And don't forget the inner fleshy artichoke heart – it's the best bit!

Above Cultivars such as 'Violetta' and 'Violet de Provence' have colourful buds.

Below While commonly harvested large as scales open (left), I prefer picking as younger tight buds called baby artichokes.

GOOD KING HENRY

EFFORT (1/5)
TASTINESS (3/5)

Blitum bonus-henricus

Good King Henry is a member of the amaranth family, the connection recognisable in the shape of its flower and seed heads. It is mainly used as a salad or cooked leaf perennial alternative to spinach, though the flavour isn't the same.

NUTRITION:
Fibre (high)
Phosphorus (moderate)
Potassium (high)
Iron (moderate)
Calcium (moderate)
Magnesium (moderate)
Vitamin A from beta-carotene (high)
Vitamin C (high)
Vitamin K (high)
Oxalic acid (moderate)
Polyphenols (high)

FAMILY: Amaranthaceae
MAX SIZE: 60cm tall, 40cm wide
GROW: spring
HARVEST: spring, summer, autumn
POT FRIENDLY: yes
SOIL: any
SITUATION: partial to full shade
HARDINESS: H5 (-15°C to -10°C)
ORIGIN: mainland Europe

Grow

In early spring or autumn, sow seeds of Good King Henry into individual 7cm pots or large, modular seed trays, about 5mm deep in compost. Cover with a transparent lid to help with humidity and leave somewhere bright such as a sunny windowsill or in an unheated polytunnel or greenhouse. I've had good germination success this way.

Once each seedling has two adult leaves in addition to the initial seed cotyledons, thin seedlings to one per pot or module. Grow on until each seedling has four to six adult leaves and roots appear out the base. At this point, usually in mid-spring, plant the seedlings in their final spot, either

Left Good King Henry is a medium sized herbaceous perennial that can tolerate shade.

in partial shade where they grow best, or in more shade if you need to. Allow 40cm space per plant.

Shade tolerance makes Good King Henry an excellent edible perennial to grow among other plants in a plant community. It doesn't mind shade cast by neighbouring plants. For instance, you can plant it behind larger perennial kale, daylily (see page 146) or beneath fruit and nut trees.

Above Young leaves can be eaten raw while larger leaves are better cooked.

Gather

An alternative name for Good King Henry is poor man's asparagus because spring shoots of this perennial can be harvested when they first appear in spring. Use in the same way by cutting off some emerging succulent shoots to the length of an asparagus spear, about 20cm, then leave other shoots to grow. You can then keep picking leaves throughout summer as you need them. Leaves can be frozen like spinach.

Eat

Good King Henry can be bitter and needs to be mixed with other flavours or cooked. It's worth including in our diets, however, for its good nutrient content, including beneficial antioxidants.

For the spring shoots, first remove the side leaves. Fry, steam or lightly boil them as you would asparagus and serve in the same way, either with butter or a drizzle of olive oil and a small amount of sea salt. Leaves can be eaten raw in salads, or cooked as you would spinach. If you find them too bitter, either soak for 30 minutes first and drain, or mask the flavour with other greens or flavourful sauces.

It is worth noting that cooking, especially boiling, will reduce the quantity of beneficial organic plant compounds found in Good King Henry. This is true of most plants. Raw or lightly steamed are probably the best ways of eating plants for maximum nutrition. It doesn't mean everything has to be raw, because cooked veg still has plenty of good nutritional benefits, but err on the side of lighter cooking to soften or reduce bitterness.

GROUND ELDER

Aegopodium podagraria

EFFORT 3/5
TASTINESS 4/5

If you can't beat it, eat it. Ground elder is one of the most unwanted plants in gardens because it spreads rapidly, swamping other perennials and is near impossible to remove. However, it is beautiful, good for wildlife, very tasty and, surprisingly, incredibly nutrient-dense. While you'll never eat ground elder into submission, if you have it, you may as well make use of it in the kitchen.

NUTRITION:
Fibre (moderate)
Protein (moderate)
Potassium (high)
Calcium (high)
Magnesium (high)
Iron (high)
Vitamin A (high)
Vitamin C (high)
Vitamin K (high)
Phytonutrients, including flavonoids (moderate)

FAMILY: Apiaceae
MAX SIZE: 50cm tall, unlimited spread
GROW: year round
HARVEST: spring, summer
POT-FRIENDLY: yes
SOIL: any
SITUATION: any
HARDINESS: H7 (< -20°C)
ORIGIN: Eurasia

Grow

If you are lucky enough not to have ground elder in your garden, don't introduce it. I can't recommend it for forage gardens because it will take over. However, there is likely a patch within walking distance, so prolific is this problem plant – and friends and neighbours would probably be delighted for you to pick its leaves.

Growing ground elder is primarily about controlling rather than care. The best method of removal is digging up its white rhizomes, which are horizontal roots that send new shoots up along their length. Once you get digging with a garden fork, the roots are easy to spot and remove. Repeat this over a growing season and you can eradicate areas of the plant. The only problem really is when ground elder grows under shrubs and trees, making it impossible to dig out all the roots. In which case, the best bet is to try and contain it. Covering for a few years with tarpaulin to exclude light also works but this takes much longer.

Left The leaves taste very mildly of sweet celery and make a tasty and nutritious base for salads.

The cultivar 'Variegatum' with snazzy, cream-edged leaves is slightly less vigorous, but not enough to contain it.

Gather

Overcome ground elder anxiety by eating its leaves. Pick young leaves that are still a lighter green to use in salads. Pick older leaves for cooking.

Below Ground elder is beautiful albeit rampant. It has a distinctive shape to the leaves and spreading growth habit but can look superficially similar to other wildflowers, including poisonous hemlock, so make sure you have a definite identification before eating.

Eat

Young leaves can be eaten raw as a salad and have a slightly mild, celery-parsley flavour. Personally I really enjoy them and would recommend people eat ground elder more often. Older leaves can be steamed, boiled or fried to use as a cooked green side dish. Leaf stems are tougher on older leaves, but are more nutrient-dense, so try to keep them on younger leaves.

Ground elder is incredibly rich in nutrients, highest in potassium, vitamin C, protein, polyphenols, and much more. Which means that while we've learned to hate this plant, we should all be re-evaluating what we think about this very useful food crop.

HOSTA

EFFORT
TASTINESS

Hosta species

Just when you think it's hard to grow vegetables in the shade, in walk hostas. Traditionally grown in the West for their ornamental leaves and flowers, hostas are all edible and across Asia they have long been used as a delicious vegetable crop.

NUTRITION:
Potassium (high)
Calcium (high)
Phosphorus (moderate)
Magnesium (moderate)
Manganese (high)
Copper (moderate)
Iron (moderate)

FAMILY: Asparagaceae
MAX SIZE: 60cm tall, 1m wide
GROW: spring, summer, autumn
HARVEST: spring, summer
POT-FRIENDLY: yes
SOIL: any
SITUATION: full to partial shade
HARDINESS: H7 (< -20°C)
ORIGIN: Asia

In gardens various species are commonly grown, such as *Hosta fortunei*, small-leaved hosta (*Hosta sieboldii*), fragrant hosta (*Hosta plantaginea*) and mountain hosta (*Hosta montana*), which have green and often variegated leaves, or Siebold's hosta (*Hosta sieboldiana*), with glaucous grey-blue leaves. There are many cultivars of these as well as hybrids of various species.

The main difference from an eating perspective is variation in nutritional content as well as the texture and thickness of the leaves. Some hostas have thicker and crunchier leaves, while others have thin, lettuce-like leaves. It's worth visiting a garden or nursery that you know has different types to see them in real life – but do ask if you want to start nibbling! No one wants to find a human bite taken out of their hostas.

Grow

Hostas grow well in full or partial shade, as long as they don't dry out completely in summer. This makes them perfect for shadier gardens or for use as a vigorous suppressing ground-cover crop in perennial edible planting, such as beneath nut and fruit trees and bushes. They can also tolerate full sun if the ground is water-retentive. However, soil does need to be quite rich in nutrients, particularly from well-rotted organic matter such as fallen leaves from nearby trees and shrubs.

Left Hosta shoots can be picked and cooked in the same way as asparagus spears.

Opposite A mature hosta patch can be full of this delicious spring vegetable.

The thickened roots of hostas are called rhizomes with the leaves growing out of a central crown. In summer hostas fire up vertical spires of flower in pale blue to white.

Being tough plants, despite their beautiful, delicate leaves, hostas can be propagated easily by division. Use a spade to slice the crown into smaller pieces to plant up elsewhere, being careful to protect as many roots as possible per growing point. They will soon grow and bulk up.

Gather

Harvest the delicious spring shoots just before or as the leaves start to unfurl at the top. Either snap them off or use a knife to slice at soil level like asparagus. More leaves will grow. Alternatively, pick leaves through the growing season, choosing the freshest-looking ones. As with most perennial crops, always keep more leaves on the plant than you pick to ensure it is able to generate energy from photosynthesis.

Eat

Hosta's star turn on the plate comes from the tightly packed leaf shoots in spring; in this form they are a bulky vegetable crop that sits alongside early-sprouting broccoli and asparagus. Sear in a frying pan for a few minutes on each side, then serve with a sprinkle of sea salt or drizzle of soy sauce. Utterly delicious!

Slice or shred the leaves as you would lettuce to use as a salad leaf – I particularly like the greener leaves for salad because they're thinner and tender. For example, 'Francee' is a decorative and tasty cultivar.

In terms of nutrition, hostas are known to be a good source of calcium and potassium, as well micronutrients manganese and iron. One study found they are slightly more nutritious than annual spring greens.

KOREAN ASTER

EFFORT
TASTINESS

Aster scaber (syn. *Doellingeria scabra*)

Widely cultivated in Korea for use in meals, Korean aster is an easy-to-grow and attractive crop with dainty, white aster flowers in late summer. The leaves, the part that is eaten, have an unusual and complex flavour which I really enjoy, somewhere between mint, oregano and something a bit more umami. To me it's reminiscent of the annual *Perilla*.

NUTRITION:
Calcium (moderate)
Iron (moderate)
Vitamin C (moderate)
Polyphenols (high)

FAMILY: Asteraceae
MAX SIZE: 1.5m tall, 1.5m wide
HARVEST: spring, summer, autumn
POT-FRIENDLY: yes
SOIL: any
SITUATION: full sun to partial shade
HARDINESS: H5 (-15°C to -10°C)
ORIGIN: China, Japan, Korea and east Russia

Left Korean aster leaves can be eaten raw but are best cooked. They have a delicious and slightly floral taste.

Grow

Korean aster is easily grown from seed sown into individual 9cm pots or seed trays of compost in spring. Sow seed on the surface of the compost, covering just slightly with a dusting of compost, and water gently from below by soaking in another tray of water. Cover with a transparent lid and leave somewhere warm, such as a sunny windowsill, or use a heated propagator in a greenhouse.

If sown in trays, after a few weeks the seedlings will germinate and can be planted into 9cm pots as their roots and leaves grow before being planted outside when they have four to six adult leaves. Plant in full sun, spacing the young plants about 50cm apart. They'll grow to about 90cm tall, including the flowers, but are airy enough to allow light in and around them to other edible perennials in a plant community.

It will take two to three years for each plant to reach mature size and they will live for many years. Once fully established, Korean aster can be divided – this can be done at any time of year but is best during the dormant period in winter. Divisions will establish full-grown plants much faster than growing from seed.

The flowers of the Korean aster are useful for pollinators as they open very late in the season when most other flowers have finished. From a design perspective, *Aster scaber* is up there with the more beautiful asters grown for ornamental purposes.

Gather

Pick leaves as needed, always keeping at least 50 per cent or more on the plant at any one time. Young leaves are tender, while mature leaves are a little tougher. Korean aster is often regarded a spring crop because the leaves are fresher then, but I've found they produce some new leaves all summer.

Eat

All leaves are edible raw, with the tender young leaves best for salads. Both young and old leaves can be cooked to wilt and soften them, making an aromatic addition to a huge range of dishes. Try slicing and steaming to stir into rice or pasta. Wrap rice or other foods with the larger leaves. When cooked, Korean aster leaves make a satisfying addition to soups, broths, ramen, stews and more.

Right The flowers make for a pretty woodland plant in mid- to late-summer.

KOREAN CELERY

EFFORT
TASTINESS

Dystaenia takeshimana

This member of the Apiaceae (formerly Umbelliferae) family from Asia is entirely edible and very tasty, which is just as well because it's a large plant that offers plenty to eat! Once mature, it will provide many a crop year round from its evergreen leaves and stems. Like perennial kale (see page 56), Korean celery is so hardy that the leaves can still be picked and used throughout winter, making it a particularly valuable crop.

NUTRITION: Despite limited credible data, it is known to contain a good amount of fibre and polyphenols, plus quantities of potassium and vitamins C and K.

FAMILY: Apiaceae
MAX SIZE: 2.5m tall, 1.5m wide
HARVEST: spring, summer, autumn
POT-FRIENDLY: no
SOIL: any
SITUATION: partial shade to full sun
HARDINESS: H7 (< -20°C)
ORIGIN: Korea

Grow

To grow from seed, sow just below the surface of compost in seed trays or individual pots in autumn or winter, and then place somewhere sheltered outside. This will give the seed a blast of cold and damp as it would experience in the wild, helping to trigger germination when the weather warms in spring, a process known as stratification which some seeds need. You can recreate this by placing the seed trays or pots in the fridge for a month or two instead.

Grow the seedlings on in individual 9cm pots until they have four to six adult leaves and plant out in their final place in spring. It's best not to move umbellifers once planted because they grow deep taproots that are damaged on lifting, so choose their spot carefully. Allow roughly 1m space or more, as they'll grow into large plants.

Korean celery grows well in partial shade to full sun, making it an excellent addition to edible plant communities either below fruit or nut trees or stuffed in among other shade-producing plants like coastal hog fennel (see page 38) and cardoon (see page 34).

Left Korean celery leaves have an aromatic flavour, which works well both in salad or when cooked.

Opposite As with many perennial edibles, it's cheap and easy to grow Korean celery from seed.

Gather

Pick leaves and young shoots. Like many plants in this book, the younger shoots are tender and the older parts a little tougher. Being a super-tough evergreen, Korean celery easily brushes off the worst winter weather, which means you only need to gather what you need as you want it.

Eat

Leaves taste a little like celery, flat-leaved parsley and lovage (see page 110-11), which they resemble, and can be used in meals where you'd like those flavours. Chop raw into salads or cook in stir-fries, or use as a garnish where parsley would normally be added. Stems can be used as you would celery, chopped and cooked in pasta sauces, stews, pies and more. For the stems, it's usually better to choose the tender young stems.

PERENNIAL KALE

EFFORT 3/5
TASTINESS 4/5

Brassica oleracea var. *ramosa*

Since I've been growing perennial kale, I have been wondering why I would still grow the annual cultivars, or at least so many of them. Perennial kale grows and tastes just like annual kale with the benefit that you don't have to sow it every year.

NUTRITION:
(based on annual kale):
Fibre (moderate)
Protein (low-moderate)
Calcium (high)
Potassium (moderate)
Phosphorus (low-moderate)
Iron (moderate)
Manganese (moderate)
Vitamin A (high)
Vitamin B9/folate (high)
Vitamin C (high, especially raw)
Vitamin E (high)
Vitamin K (high)

FAMILY: Brassicaceae
MAX SIZE: 100cm tall, 80cm wide
HARVEST: year round
POT-FRIENDLY: yes
SOIL: nutrient-rich
SITUATION: full sun to partial shade
HARDINESS: H7 (< -20°C)
ORIGIN: Britain, France and Spain

Above A cutting of 'Daubenton's Variegata', a very ornamental kale that's slightly slower growing because it has less chlorophyll in the leaves.

Opposite 'Taunton Deane' is stockier than other cultivars, better able to withstand strong gusts in this windtunnel between buildings.

Grow

Perennial kale is usually sold as rooted or rootless cuttings. Take 10–15cm cuttings yourself, cutting side shoots from a friend's plant. Remove the lower two-thirds of the cutting's leaves and poke the lower half into individual 7–9cm-wide pots of compost, watering lightly. Place somewhere warm and sunny, such as a windowsill, at any time of year. Roots will form within two to four weeks and new leaves will begin growing. When roots appear out the bottom of the pots, the young plants will be ready to plant outside in spring or summer.

Space perennial kales 80cm apart. When large, all kales can be top-heavy with lush growth, so support them against strong winds with wooden stakes, tying them in gently with twine. You may need to cover plants with insect mesh in summer to block white butterflies from laying eggs on them and pigeons or pheasants eating the leaves. Otherwise, kale is a trouble-free crop. Kale can attract aphids, but these are easily brushed off perennial kale, which is usually smooth-leaved.

Taste is very similar between all cultivars. 'Taunton Deane' is bushier with multiple stems and shorter at 1.2m, useful in windy areas and requiring less to no support. 'Purple Tree Collard' is supersized to 1.8m tall and has large leaves, and these require staking to protect against wind. 'Daubenton' and 'Daubenton's Variegata' are on the stockier side. See also sea kale on page 58.

Plants should live for up to 10 years, but it's always advisable to take some cuttings in late summer or autumn as backups in case plants are damaged by winter wind or wet. You can collect and sow their seeds which will lead to interesting variations – you can try breeding your own, but they may not be the same as the parent plants.

All brassicas can be affected by clubroot, a soil-borne pathogen, making it sensible to rotate the growing beds after a number of years. Thanks to perennial kale's longer lifespan, rotating beds every 8–10 years means it's unlikely clubroot would survive for that time without the plants. It spreads only in the soil, so cuttings taken from high up the plant will be safe.

Tip

Annual kale will behave like a perennial by self-sowing each year if you let it flower – I do this with the cultivar 'Russian Red'.

Gather

Cut leaves at the base of leaf stems (petiole) using scissors or secateurs. Eat fresh or store in bags or tubs in the fridge for a few days. Cut along the edge of leaf stems if tough and keep only the leafy parts.

Eat

All leaves are edible. Young leaves are delicious raw in salads and sandwiches, while the older large leaves are best cooked. Perennial kale is as nutritious as annual cultivars, particularly useful for iron, calcium and magnesium. Kale is such a healthy way of obtaining essential nutrients that I try to include it in as many meals as possible. Our bodies access nutrients best if eaten whole or chopped up rather than always whizzed to a liquid in smoothies.

SEA KALE

EFFORT 1/5
TASTINESS 4/5

Crambe maritima

Found naturally along coasts on sandy or stony beaches and nearby, sea kale has beautiful, silver-glaucous leaves, tinged purple when they first emerge in spring. Sea kale tastes different to other types of kale and grows in a different way. It's a very ornamental foliage plant.

NUTRITION: Despite limited credible data, it is known to be very high in vitamin C and polyphenols, with good amounts of vitamin A, sugars and other vitamins and minerals. Comparable to, or potentially more nutrient-dense than, other kales.

FAMILY: Brassicaceae
MAX SIZE: 75cm tall, 60cm wide
GROW: spring
HARVEST: spring, summer
POT-FRIENDLY: yes
SOIL: free-draining
SITUATION: full sun
HARDINESS: H7 (< -20°C)
ORIGIN: Europe to Caucasus

Grow

Despite the name, sea kale can grow anywhere in a temperate climate. One of the key differences to other types of kale is that sea kale sends up multiple shoots from a ground-level crown, rather than one or two main stems that grow tall and top-heavy. This more compact and dense growth makes sea kale tolerant of exposed sites, as it evolved living by the sea! When I was speaking to our neighbour June Eaton (see interview on page 176), we were both delighted to spot little seedlings around the base of her three-year-old sea kale. Crops that self-sow naturally, without dominating, are added to my 'gold dust' plant list. It's an especially valuable trait in plant community design because it helps make the community self-sustaining for many generations to come.

Sea kale is easiest grown from seed, which you can collect for free from wild plants, being sure to take only a few, leaving most for the wild. Sow the seed into 7cm pots or seed trays of compost 1cm deep in spring, water lightly, and it'll soon germinate. When large enough, plant the seedlings in their permanent spot 60–80cm apart.

Gather

With established sea kale you can cover emerging leaves in late winter using an upturned bucket or terracotta rhubarb forcer. Victorians used to have

Left Sea kale leaves are so large that you only need a few for a generous (and very tasty) portion of cooked greens.

Opposite Unlike other perennial kale with stems, sea kale grows many shoots from a ground-level crown, useful for windy spots.

dedicated terracotta sea kale forcers for this purpose. Blocking sunlight blanches the stems, making them pale and sweet as they stretch upwards searching for light. These white shoots can be snapped off easily at a length of about 25cm. Once harvested, remove the forcer and allow at least a third of the leaves to produce energy for the plant.

Later in the year, use scissors or secateurs to cut green leaves at the base of leaf stems (petioles). Eat fresh or cover and store in the fridge for a few days. In late summer, you can also snap off the flower-buds before they open and use them like sprouting broccoli.

Eat

To me, sea kale tastes less like a brassica – it's fresher and more succulent, perhaps a little like asparagus. Try some to see what you think. That said, it is cooked and used in the same way as any cooked green: steamed, boiled or fried. Young leaves can be eaten raw.

SMALL-LEAVED LIME TREE

Tilia cordata

EFFORT ●●●○○
TASTINESS ●●●○○

Money may not grow on trees but food does. Trees that provide regular crops of salad leaves are a dream for food production, and lime trees in the *Tilia* genus are one of the best. All trees in the *Tilia* genus have edible leaves, sap and flowers. *Tilia cordata* is a preferred species for its smooth and tasty young leaves, and it's my favourite for that reason. Although they are called lime trees, they are not related to trees that produced lime fruit (*Citrus × aurantiifolia*).

NUTRITION:
Fibre (moderate)
Calcium (moderate)
Magnesium (moderate)
Potassium (moderate)
Phosphorus (moderate)
Iron (moderate)
Zinc (moderate)
Vitamin C (low)
Polyphenols, including flavonoids (high)

FAMILY: Malvaceae
MAX SIZE: 20m tall, 20m wide (can be coppiced)
GROW: winter, spring
HARVEST: spring
POT-FRIENDLY: no
SOIL: any
SITUATION: full sun to partial shade
HARDINESS: H6 (-20°C to -15°C)
ORIGIN: Europe to central Siberia

Grow

Tilia cordata (and all lime trees in the genus) want to grow into a huge deciduous tree, growing upward of 20m tall and wide. They need full sunlight to grow well, as well as soil that doesn't dry out in summer.

Large lime trees can produce emergent shoots at the base of their trunk called suckers, from which we can forage leaves. However, in gardens it's easier and more practical to keep the tree small, either through coppicing every few years, regular picking (see below) or planting as a hedge that can be clipped to size. Like most wild deciduous trees, *Tilia* species will respond to being cut back in winter with young shoots below the cut. By coppicing *Tilia* it's possible to keep it the size of a small shrub. You can even pollard, which means to cut the main trunk and branches higher up. By cutting the main trunk at 1.5–2m, you can grow a column of shoots that keep regrowing for harvest. This also makes it easy to grow other salad crops beneath and around the clipped *Tilia*. When the *Tilia* leaves drop in autumn, they then feed the soil around it and the other crops.

Gather

Pick the newest leaves by hand when they look slightly transparent and succulent, as these will be the nicest to eat. As with cut-and-come-again lettuce, you can pick what you want as you need it.

At the same time as harvesting the leaves, snip off a few ends of young shoots to another growing point (leaf node). This will encourage new shoots from the other growing points, producing even more leaves. Keep picking and snipping through the season, making sure there are plenty of leaves on the tree at any one time to produce energy from photosynthesis.

Eat

Tilia leaves are mainly used as a raw leaf in salads and sandwiches, although they can be added to dishes too, so have a play to see what you think.

It's been found that *Tilia cordata* can absorb too much metal content from soils. If then eaten in large quantities, that can be harmful to us. It's recommended you grow and eat leaves primarily from rural areas that are less at risk of excess metals from pollution and to test soil for harmful metal levels to be sure. Though this is true of all crops really, making soil testing important.

Right Saplings of this common tree are inexpensive and easy to grow.

Opposite Pick leaves young and translucent while they are still tender.

SORREL

EFFORT
TASTINESS

Rumex acetosa

Sorrel is a wild plant of grasslands and one of the main food plants eaten by the caterpillar of the small copper butterfly (*Lycaena phlaeas*), among many other insects. It's also a tasty, nutrient-packed perennial salad leaf or cooked green. Leaves contain oxalic acid, which can be reduced through cooking or diluted among other ingredients.

NUTRITION:
Calcium (moderate)
Iron (moderate)
Provitamin A (moderate)
Vitamin C (high)
Polyphenols (moderate)

FAMILY: Polygonaceae
MAX SIZE: 30cm tall, 30cm wide
GROW: spring, summer, autumn
HARVEST: year round
POT-FRIENDLY: yes
SOIL: any
SITUATION: full sun
HARDINESS: H7 (< -20°C)
ORIGIN: temperate Eurasia and Morocco

Sorrel is a useful, high-yielding and resilient crop that is worth cultivating – plant breeders could explore breeding sorrel cultivars with a lower oxalic acid content, for example. As a wild plant not commonly sold in shops, there is limited nutritional data available for sorrel from credible sources.

Grow

Sorrel grows well in dense grassland, which is all the information we need to tell us it will also grow easily among the competition of other low-growing crops in edible plant communities. Its key requirement is full sunlight. If it becomes too shaded by larger shrubs or trees, it won't grow as strongly.

Sow seeds slightly below the surface of soil where you want sorrel to grow, allowing a 20cm space per plant. Or start them off in 9cm pots of compost, planting out later. If you leave the flower stalks to set seed, they will produce new seedlings around the place without completely taking over.

A long-lived perennial, sorrel will come back year after year. Even in the worst winter weather its evergreen leaves can still be seen and gathered.

One study suggests the close relation *Rumex sanguineus*, also known as bloody or red-veined dock, may have a slightly lower oxalic acid content.

Gather

Pick leaves as required. Younger leaves are sweeter and more tender.

Left Sorrel leaves have a vibrant, green colour to them.

Eat

Sorrel contains oxalic acid, giving it's a slightly sour, lemony taste, which is part of the appeal. This is perfectly safe in occasional and small quantities. Though for some people – including me – oxalic-acid-rich plants eaten raw can make the throat feel sore.

Include a few leaves in salads or sandwiches rather than on their own to minimise the impact, as this dilutes the leaves in a mix with other ingredients. Cooking sorrel is another good option because this significantly reduces the oxalic acid – especially if boiled in water and drained, as much of the oxalic acid is removed in the water.

People who have renal problems or are susceptible to kidney stones should avoid eating lots of sorrel as a precaution because the oxalic acid can make these conditions worse. In addition, sorrel can over-accumulate metals to levels that may be a risk in metal-heavy soils, making it worth a professional soil analysis to check yours.

Above Sorrel supports many insects and is the primary food source of the small copper butterfly.

Below Sorrel leaves are edible at any stage but, as with many wild forageable plants, are mild and tender when young.

STONECROP/ORPINE

EFFORT 1/5
TASTINESS 4/5

Hylotelephium spectabile and *Hylotelephium telephium*

Hylotelephium (formerly *Sedum*) are particularly useful edible plants. Their fleshy stems and leaves mean they are drought tolerant, which is useful in dry summers. They're also tolerant of wet and cold, as long as the soil isn't completely waterlogged. I've also found they cope with some shade and will self-sow.

NUTRITION:
Despite limited credible data, peer-reviewed studies found both stonecrop and orpine contain notable amounts of calcium, potassium, magnesium, and the antioxidant polyphenols quercetin and kaempferol.

FAMILY: Crassulaceae
MAX SIZE: 50cm tall, 50cm wide
GROW: spring, summer
HARVEST: spring, summer, autumn
POT-FRIENDLY: yes
SOIL: any
SITUATION: full sun
HARDINESS: H7 (< -20°C)
ORIGIN: east Asia (*Hylotelephium spectabile*), Europe across to Russia and north China (*Hylotelephium telephium*)

The flowers add a burst of colour in summer and are extremely useful for pollinating insects. And did I mention they're one of my favourite perennial salad leaves? While they aren't packed with flavour, to me they have a comparable mild taste and texture to crunchy lettuce, making them an excellent leaf to bulk up salads.

Grow

Not all *Hylotelephium* are edible. However, the straight species of both stonecrop (*Hylotelephium spectabile*) and orpine (*Hylotelephium telephium*) are safe and tasty. These have green to purple leaves and pink flowers. I recommend sourcing your plants from reliable suppliers who can confirm they are the edible species. Other *Hylotelephium* species and some cultivars are edible, but it's better to treat these with caution until more advice confirms this.

Hylotelephium are incredibly easy to grow across various climates. All they need is sun and a free-draining soil that is fairly fertile. In practice, I've found they are very resilient, growing in sandy, free-draining soil in southern England as well as clay-loam water-retentive, very fertile soil in the North.

They can be grown from seed sown in spring onto the surface of compost in trays, transplanting them into individual 9cm pots when they have four to six leaves. Alternatively, they are very easy to grow from stem or leaf cuttings, and this method guarantees they will be genetic clones of the parent plant.

For stem cuttings, snip off a 10cm length of stem before it starts forming flower-buds in early summer. Remove the lower two-thirds of leaves and poke the lower half of the stem into a 9cm pot of compost (one stem per pot). There is no need to cover. Simply place somewhere bright and warm out of direct sunlight – such as a slightly shaded part of a patio or greenhouse – and the cuttings will root in a matter of weeks.

Leaf cuttings are like magic. This method doesn't work on all plant species, but with *Hylotelephium* this is a good way to grow lots of plants. Pick off a handful of large, healthy leaves from the stem, then poke the lower third of the leaf into a tray or 9cm pot of compost (five to seven leaves per pot). It is worth covering the pots with a transparent lid or sealable plastic bag to retain humidity. Place somewhere bright and warm, and these leaves too will root! After a time, little leaves will grow from the base of the cuttings. Plant into individual 9cm pots when they do.

Above *Hylotelephium* grow beautiful mid- to late-summer flowers that are loved by pollinators and garden designers alike.

Right Some plants can be grown easily from leaf cuttings that then sprout roots and shoots.

Opposite Pinch off the main growing point or cut a stem by a third and many new shoots will grow with more leaves to eat.

Gather

Pick leaves from the stem as needed, leaving at least 50 per cent on the plant. Pinch off the top of the main stem early in summer to force side shoots to grow, and thus more leaves.

Eat

Add leaves raw to salads either whole or chopped. Excellent as a base with more flavoursome leaves such as wild rocket. Leaves and young stems can also be sautéed.

SUNCHOKE

EFFORT 1/5
TASTINESS 4/5

Helianthus tuberosus

Sweet and nutty, with a flavour reminiscent of the globe artichoke from which it gets its name (see page 44), sunchokes are one of my favourite-tasting root vegetables. Often called Jerusalem artichokes, they have nothing to do with Jerusalem. They were first cultivated by the Indigenous people of the northern Americas, before colonialists took some back to Europe.

NUTRITION:
Carbohydrate (moderate)
Fibre (moderate)
Inulin (high)
Potassium (moderate)
Copper (moderate)
Polyphenols (moderate)

FAMILY: Asteraceae
MAX SIZE: 2.5m tall, 50cm wide
HARVEST: autumn
POT-FRIENDLY: yes
SOIL: any free-draining
SITUATION: full sun
HARDINESS: H5 (-15°C to -10°C)
ORIGIN: Central and East Canada and the USA

Grow

Sunchokes couldn't be easier to grow, and they're an excellent perennial crop. In spring, plant tubers on their sides in a sunny spot, 15cm deep and 30cm apart. I've grown them on sandy, free-draining soil and heavy clay, and they performed the same for me. 'Fuseau' is a widely available cultivar with smooth tubers, making them easier to clean. 'Dwarf Sunray' is slightly shorter, growing to 1.8m.

A hardy perennial member of the Asteraceae (sunflower family), sunchokes rapidly grow well over head height in summer. Super sturdy, they need no supports, no feeding or watering, and very little

weeding as they'll outgrow everything. They have small, yellow flowers in autumn, which are pretty and useful for pollinators when fewer flowers are around.

In fact, the only thing you have to worry about is that they can be *too* vigorous, slowly spreading from their tubers over the years – making it important that you dig them up to eat!

Gather

From autumn through winter, dig tubers as needed, composting the above-ground plant material – the plants die back over winter. Sunchokes can be stored in the fridge for a short time, or longer in trays of damp sand in a shed or garage. Personally, I find it easier to leave the tubers in the ground to gather when we want them. For each plant, lift all tubers and replant one in the same spot for next year.

Eat

Scrub any soil off the tubers and eat them with or without the thin skin, either raw or cooked. Roast, sauté, fry, boil, steam, ferment, or turn into a purée or soup. Sunchokes have a fantastically rich flavour – I love them roasted or as a purée accompaniment.

A good source of carbohydrates and inulin, sunchokes are thought to improve blood pressure, inflammation and heart health. Inulin is a type of soluble prebiotic fibre that can be extremely good for our intestinal microbiota because it stimulates the growth of beneficial bacteria. Stimulation of bacteria from the inulin can cause an increase in gases, however, which can be uncomfortable for some. Eating a little and often is the answer, to see how our bodies react by not overloading the intestines with too much inulin in one go, helping our bodies to become accustomed.

I like to add two or three tubers to a mix of roast vegetables, stir-fries, pies, curries or stews to include their flavour while diluting the inulin per meal. I never notice any difference when using them in this way, enjoying their delicious taste and health benefits.

Right A perennial member of the sunflower family, sunchokes even produce miniature yellow sunflowers in autumn.

Opposite Sunchoke 'Fuseau' is slightly smoother and doesn't need peeling, though if you want to the knobbly bits snap off very easily first.

WELSH ONION

EFFORT
TASTINESS

Allium fistulosum

Various bee species can be seen rummaging around Welsh onion flowers in early summer – a perfect example of food crops also supporting wildlife. Being a perennial, pollinators have a stable food source they can rely on every year from this taste powerhouse.

NUTRITION:
(based on other leafy annual onions):
Iron (moderate)
Vitamin A (moderate)
Vitamin B9/folate (high)
Vitamin C (moderate)
Vitamin K (high)
Phytonutrients (high)

FAMILY: Amaryllidaceae
MAX SIZE: 50cm tall, 20cm wide
GROW: spring
HARVEST: year round
POT-FRIENDLY: yes
SOIL: any free-draining
SITUATION: full sun
HARDINESS: H4 (-10°C to -5°C)
ORIGIN: cultigen from China

Welsh onion is an odd name for *Allium fistulosum* because they have no connection with Wales. In fact, they are a cultigen from China, which is a species known only in cultivation with no wild ancestor. It's hard to confirm exactly how the Welsh onion gained its common name, but there are records from the seventeenth century in Germany in which it was called *welsche*, meaning 'foreign'.

Grow

Welsh onions are so easy to grow from seed that it is the main method I'd recommend. A packet of seed allows you to grow hundreds of plants. Sow the seeds in spring, 1cm apart on top of a seed tray of compost, covering the seeds in a light dusting of compost. Water gently by soaking the tray from below or use a very fine watering can rose to prevent the seeds washing around. Cover with a transparent lid and place somewhere warm, such as a windowsill, until the seeds germinate in a week or two.

Once the seedlings have two to three leaves, move outside to acclimatise to colder weather for a few weeks – don't worry, they are hardy. Then plant the seedlings into their final position outside as the spring weather warms, giving each onion 20–30cm space. They may look small, but eventually Welsh onions bunch up into a clump similar to chives but with chunkier, taller leaves. Keep watered until the plants appear well established, at which point they will become drought tolerant.

Left These highly nutritious leaves can be used in any dish where you want a sweet onion flavour.

Above Welsh onions are a doddle to grow from seed, here I've grown hundreds of plants from one seed packet.

Right Flowering in early summer, pale Welsh onion flowers are architectural and absolutely loved by pollinators.

There are red and white versions of Welsh onion, but I've found they grow in exactly the same way and taste the same. It's just useful to have a choice of colour for salads.

In time, Welsh onions multiply by producing more bulbs. Once they do this, you can lift and divide the clump to produce more clumps around your garden. They will also flower, giving you a chance to collect your own seed.

Gather

All of the plant is edible; however, we mainly eat the green leaves because Welsh onions only form a shallot sized bulb. Having said that, if you have lots of Welsh onions you can, of course, lift some out to use the bulbs. Leave enough plants in the ground for future crops. Harvesting leaves is very easy: cut near the base with scissors or secateurs, or you can even just tear them off with your hands. New leaves will grow.

Eat

Chop leaves to use raw in salads or cooked in stir-fries, stews and other meals as you would onion, leek or spring onion. Experiment with your favourite dishes to see how many Welsh onion leaves you need in comparison to a regular bulb onion to create similar flavours. Green onion leaves tend to have different nutritional components to the white bulb, often with more vitamins and minerals, such as vitamin C, iron, folate and calcium, plus antioxidant carotenoids and flavonoids.

WILD ROCKET

EFFORT (1 of 5)
TASTINESS (3 of 5)

Diplotaxis tenuifolia

Wild rocket is a perennial with a stronger flavour than its cultivated relation, the annual rocket sold in shops. Cultivated crops have generally been bred for sweetness over the years. However, the rockets don't differ that much, especially when mixed into salads, sandwiches or other dishes. In fact, the extra flavour of wild rocket could be seen as a bonus.

NUTRITION:
Fibre (moderate)
Calcium (moderate)
Iron (moderate)
Potassium (moderate)
Vitamin A (moderate)
Vitamin B9/folate (moderate)
Vitamin C (moderate)
Vitamin K (high)
Beta-carotene (moderate)
Polyphenols, including flavonoids (moderate)

FAMILY: Brassicaceae
MAX SIZE: 30cm tall, 30cm wide
HARVEST: year round
POT-FRIENDLY: yes
SOIL: any
SITUATION: full sun
HARDINESS: H4 (-10°C to -5°C)
ORIGIN: western mainland Europe to Mediterranean

Grow

Easily grown from seed, wild rocket can be sown directly in the ground or in 7–9cm pots of compost. Sow seeds about 1cm deep in full sun, where they will grow best. Water well and the seeds will germinate freely in a week or two. Plants should be spaced about 20–30cm apart, remove weaker seedlings thin out rows.

As a perennial, wild rocket lives for years. It's useful in a low-growing salad crop plant community alongside scorzonera (see page 42), *Hylotelephium* (see page 64) and other crops of similar size.

Allow to flower and set seed and new plants will pop up by themselves, giving you unlimited rocket leaves forever! I love this about edible plant communities: if we get the mix right, they will self-propagate with new plants, while blocking out any interlopers we don't want growing in that spot. Much better than high-maintenance rows of annual planting.

Wild rocket is fully hardy, but its leaves can become tatty as growth slows during winter. Grow some wild rocket in a sheltered spot or cover with a cloche or horticultural fleece and you should have some leaves to pick in the colder months.

Keep watered for a milder flavour, as the leaves can become very fiery during hot, dry spells.

Gather

As easy as picking leaves. Younger leaves are a little milder in flavour and sweeter, while older leaves are stronger and coarser. Flowers are also edible with a good kick. Always keep some leaves on the plant to power new growth. The more you pick, the more leaves will grow.

Left These wild rocket plants were grown from seed in spring and will return each year as well as set seed around the parent plants for even more leaves.

Eat

I've downgraded rocket's tastiness because while it certainly has a good flavour, on its own I personally find this can be very strong, which I find true of the annual shop-bought stuff too. However, I appreciate many people love rocket's kick, so give it an extra point or two for flavour if that includes you.

I like to mix wild rocket with milder leaves, including scorzonera (*Reichardia picroides*) and lime tree (see page 60), where its strong flavour becomes a delicious part of the mix rather than overpowering it. A little drizzle of good-quality olive oil with a small sprinkle of sea salt or balsamic vinegar can also work well with rocket. Older leaves can be wilted as part of cooked dishes, making them more palatable.

Above Wild rocket leaves can be picked through the season for salad with a peppery kick.

OTHER PERENNIAL VEGETABLES WORTH A TRY

- Babington leeks *Allium ampeloprasum* var. *babingtonii*
- Earth chestnut *Bunium bulbocastanum*
- Oca *Oxalis tuberosa*
- Olives *Olea europaea*
- Potato bean climber *Apios americana*
- Salad burnet *Sanguisorba minor*
- Skirret *Sium sisarum*
- Sneezewort *Achillea ptarmica*
- Stinging nettle *Urtica dioica*
- Sweet yarrow *Achillea ageratum*
- Watercress *Nasturtium officinale*
- Yacon *Smallanthus sonchifolius*

Fruit

Fruit plants are the stalwarts of forage gardens, growing with little or no input from us except to pick and eat. Perhaps an occasional prune. Many, including gooseberry and rhubarb, are tolerant of partial shade, making them useful in urban gardens and under taller trees. In fact, most of the fruit we eat grows on perennial plants, adding a designer beauty, so are worth planting for their looks and wildlife value alone. Every garden should have at least one fruit tree, bush, climber or small perennial for the blossom and colourful fruit. But more than that, fresh fruit is a fantastic source of vitamins, fibre and antioxidants, which help reduce the risk of serious diseases. Many cultivars available to gardeners are so sweet that they compare to shop-bought confectionery, but they are so much better for us and the planet.

Above Wild strawberries, *Fragaria vesca*, spread themselves by stolons, above-ground runners, and seed needing no looking after. While these tiny fruits aren't very filling, they are a sweet treat to forage.

APPLE

EFFORT 3/5
TASTINESS 5/5

Malus × domestica

Professor Povey (see page 182) at Leeds University's School of Food Science and Nutrition pointed out that apples are one of the best fruits to eat for polyphenols, including quercetin, catechin and phloridzin.

NUTRITION:
Carbohydrate (moderate)
Fibre (moderate)
Potassium (moderate)
Vitamin C (moderate)
Polyphenols (high)

FAMILY: Rosaceae
MAX SIZE: 4m tall, 4m wide (pruned)
GROW: winter, spring
HARVEST: early summer
POT-FRIENDLY: on M27 and M9 rootstocks only
SOIL: any
SITUATION: full sun to dappled shade
HARDINESS: H6 (-20°C to -15°C)
ORIGIN: Central Asia

Above Perfect crispy 'Falstaff' apples from my allotment grown on a single stepover tree pruned to 1.2m wide by 50cm tall.

Apples contain more polyphenols within their fibre that our bodies can freely use than many other fruits. They are also a source of carbohydrates, vitamin C, potassium and low levels of many other nutrients. As Professor Povey says, 'An apple a day really does keep the doctor away.'

Grow

Apple trees are easy to grow in almost any temperate garden. First, decide which cultivars you like to eat versus the cultivars that are disease-resistant and will grow best in your area. Always speak to your nearest fruit specialist nursery or orchard, as they will have the best recommendations for your region. Second, all apple cultivars are available on different rootstocks, which determines how big and vigorous the tree will be. M27 grows to 2m; M9 is slightly more vigorous, growing to 2.3m; M26 grows to around 3m and is a good intercropping size; MM106 grows up to 4m; and M25 is large at 5m-plus.

I've had good success in southern and northern England with 'Katy' and 'Red Falstaff'. Hardier varieties cropping well for me on our exposed farm are 'Annie Elizabeth', 'James Grieve' and 'Lord Derby'. Prune apple trees in winter while dormant to remove any damaged, diseased or rubbing branches. Many advise keeping an open goblet structure to branches, but they will crop regardless. Reduce clusters of apples to no more than three in mid-summer for better fruit.

Gather

Apples are ripe in autumn when the stalk comes away easily from the tree as you lift the fruit upwards. Collect gently, so as not to bruise the apples, and store carefully in trays, making sure they aren't touching, which can encourage rot and mould. Store apples in a cold, dark pantry, shed or garage that is dry and protected from marauding animals. Depending on the cultivar, they can keep and be used through most of winter in this way.

Eat

Dessert apple cultivars are those you can eat raw straight from the tree. Be sure to eat the skin, as it contains many nutrients. Cooking apples are best heated in pies or stewed, which can then be frozen (or gobbled up immediately).

Below 'James Grieve' ripens later than others in autumn and stores well, grown among dense planting in our garden.

Right 'Discovery', also growing in our garden, is the first of our apples to ripen with a pink blush to its flesh.

BILBERRY

Vaccinium myrtillus

EFFORT 2/5
TASTINESS 4/5

When we first moved into our home next to moorland, we soon heard about the joys of picking bilberries in summer from our neighbours. The bilberry is a wild shrub with berries that resemble a darker, smaller version of the related blueberry.

NUTRITION:
Carbohydrate (moderate)
Fibre (moderate)
Manganese (moderate)
Vitamin C (moderate)
Vitamin K (moderate)
Polyphenols, including anthocyanins (high)

FAMILY: Ericaceae
MAX SIZE: 40cm tall, 40cm wide

HARVEST: mid-summer
POT-FRIENDLY: yes
SOIL: acidic
SITUATION: full sun to partial shade
HARDINESS: H6 (-20°C to -15°C)
ORIGIN: Greenland, temperate Eurasia, West Canada and West USA

On tasting a bilberry for the first time my mind was blown that they're almost exactly like their expensive relation. Yet here they were, growing for free all across temperate parts of the Northern Hemisphere.

Grow

Bilberries need acidic soil to grow, and they're found in the wild on nutrient-poor acidic soils on peatland moors. I have seen them growing happily in partial shade but to fruit well, they do need full sun.

If you have free-draining acidic soil, you can grow bilberries in your garden. Each plant only produces a handful of berries sparsely across its branches, so you will need a good number of plants for a worthwhile crop.

Slow growers, it can take quite a few years for bilberries to mature. Once established, however, they will produce berries every year with no involvement from you. No pruning, fertilising or watering required.

It is possible to grow bilberries in large 40cm pots of ericaceous compost (which is formulated for acid-loving plants), but due to the number of plants needed, you'd need a lot of pots! It may be better to find a local wild patch to pick from instead.

Left Foraging teacher Kasia Ka gathering bilberries on the sunny moors above our house before her students joined her.

Gather

Bilberry bushes can be identified by their 30–40cm size, wiry stems (which are green until they turn woody), and small, oval, shiny leaves. Bilberries first appear red before turning a dark purple. They are ripe when about 1cm in size, dark and noticeably softer when given a squeeze.

You can buy hand-held rakes that look like miniature dustpans with spokes to sweep through bilberry bushes, collecting the fruit. However, these tend to collect unripe berries and damage the plants, tearing off stems and leaves that you have to pick out anyway. I prefer to pick bilberries by hand because I enjoy this and the ripe berries come away easily.

The fruits are non-climacteric, which means they won't ripen once picked, so leave any unripe bilberries on the plants to pick later. Bilberry juice and flesh is a deep inky red, so be prepared for your fingers to get stained!

Tip

If you prefer regular blueberries, they grow in exactly the same way as bilberries.

Eat

You can eat bilberries ripe from the bush. I often eat them when out for a walk on the moors, picking and nibbling as I go. They are dense with goodness, including various vitamins and antioxidants from the anthocyanins that give them their deep red colour. They taste just a tiny bit more acidic and have a slightly more fibrous texture than blueberries, but they are still sweet and delicious.

Bilberries can be used to make drinks and pies. While out photographing bilberries I bumped into forager Kasia Ka with a group of students whom she was teaching. Kasia told me about the Polish dumplings she was going to make, known as *pierogi z jagodami*. The dumplings are filled with savoury ingredients like potato as well as the bilberries, and eaten as a main course rather than a sweet desert.

Above Bilberries look and taste very similar to their relative blueberries. They are ripe when dark blue.

BLACKBERRY

EFFORT ●●○○○
TASTINESS ●●●●●

Rubus fruticosus

Blackberries grow everywhere, so we could all be saving lots of money in summer by seeking our nearest wild plants to forage for free. Sun-warmed fresh blackberries are extra sweet and delicious. They're also healthy sweet treats that are low in calories but contain fibre, manganese, vitamins C and K, folate (vitamin B9) and polyphenols.

NUTRITION:
Fibre (high)
Manganese (high)
Copper (moderate)
Vitamin B9/folate (moderate)
Vitamin C (high)
Vitamin E (moderate)
Vitamin K (high)
Polyphenols (high)

FAMILY: Rosaceae
MAX SIZE: 2.5m tall, 2.5m wide
GROW: winter, spring
HARVEST: mid-summer
POT-FRIENDLY: no
SOIL: any
SITUATION: full sun
HARDINESS: H6 (-20°C to -15°C)
ORIGIN: northern and central Europe

Above Nothing beats a delicious plateful of freshly gathered blackberries, foraged from your garden or a nearby hedge.

Opposite Blackberries ripen in succession over a number of weeks in mid-summer allowing you to go back every day for the ripest dark blackberries.

Grow

Although the wild species is a prolific fruiter already, cultivars have been bred for stems without their vicious spines and for larger, even sweeter fruit. For this reason, in gardens I have to recommend choosing a cultivar.

Two cultivars given the RHS Award of Garden Merit (meaning they've been tested under trial conditions) are 'Loch Ness', which grows to 2m tall and wide, and the slightly more compact 'Loch Tay', growing to 1.5m. Their names offer a clue to how hardy blackberries are, growing very well in Scotland's climate where these cultivars were bred.

New blackberry stems grow in the first year, then flower and fruit in the second year. The only effort required for growing blackberries is pruning out the old stems that fruited at the base in winter while the plant is dormant. You can make this scrambling plant easier to manage and people usually tie the new stems horizontally along free-standing wires or against a wall. Training blackberries in this way makes it easier and quicker to gather the berries in summer.

Buy cultivars as bareroot plants while they are dormant in winter – bareroot means with no soil. Plant immediately in a spot that allows 2–3m room for growth. In a plant community system, blackberries are best planted somewhere that receives full sun for better fruiting, such as on the edge of a forest garden or against a sunny fence or wall.

It's possible to propagate cultivars by burying or pegging the end of a new stem to the ground, keeping the very tip above ground. The tip will soon root, at which point you can cut it away from the parent plant and move into a pot or another spot. This easy technique works with lots of other plants – give it a go!

Gather

Blackberries crop over a number of weeks from mid-summer. Pick them regularly once ripe to beat the birds to it, as they love a tasty blackberry too.

Eat

Eat blackberries fresh in desserts with yoghurt or ice cream, use them to make jam or in bakes, or freeze them for later use at home.

CLIMBING FRUIT

EFFORT 4/5
TASTINESS 5/5

Various species

Climbing plants are incredibly useful for maximising vertical space, and thanks to modern breeding, certain cultivars of climbing fruits, such as dessert grapes, can crop in cooler climates. Grow climbing fruit up walls or fences using trellis or climbing wires for deliciously attractive large plants.

All three of the climbing fruit described contain a range of different nutrients. Grapes are high in natural sugars, vitamin K and antioxidant flavonoid polyphenols, moderate potassium. Kiwi fruit is high in fibre, vitamin C, vitamin K, potassium and polyphenols (higher antioxidants in kiwi berries because skin is eaten). Akebia pulp is moderate in fibre and potassium, with too little research into the skins.

FAMILY: Various
MAX SIZE: 8m high, 8m wide (contained with pruning)
GROW: spring
HARVEST: summer, autumn
POT-FRIENDLY: no
SOIL: any
SITUATION: full sun (partial shade for Akebia)
HARDINESS: Chocolate vines H6 (-20°C to -15°C), grapes H5 (-15°C to -10°C), kiwi H4 (-10°C to -5°C)
ORIGIN: various

Grow

Grapes (*Vitis vinifera*) with seeds in them tend to be a little better at ripening in cooler climates, but personally I find them irritating to eat, so I prefer hardy seedless cultivars such as 'Lakemont', 'Suffolk Red', 'Vanessa' and 'Flame'. Plant in spring in your sunniest, warmest spot and grow up a trellis, pergola or supports. The easiest way to prune grapes is to have one main trunk to about 1.5m, and then let it produce one or two horizontal fruiting arms. These grow in the first year, then fruit in the next. Once fruited, remove that arm entirely while allowing a replacement arm to grow for next year.

Kiwi fruits seem exotic but are hardy and will fruit in cooler climates. The large fruited *Actinidia deliciosa* needs a male and female plant, so if you have room, grow one of each. If you only have space for one, grow smaller-fruited, self-fertile 'Jenny'. Kiwi berries, *Actinidia arguta*, are grape-size kiwis and 'Issai' is self-fertile.

Akebia quinata and *Akebia longeracemosa*, the chocolate vines, both produce similar purple fruit and need two vines to cross-pollinate, otherwise you'll mainly have their beautiful spring flowers. Plant in partial shade.

Below Although these grapes are growing in a greenhouse, there are many hardy cultivars today that thrive and crop outdoors.

All of these are vigorous, large climbers that need lots of space or regular pruning to contain them, otherwise they'll grow up to 8m tall and wide, lifting their fruit out of reach. For this reason, it can be handy to grow them on wires on a wall or fence, or over pergolas where you can train and contain their stems to keep fruit within arm's reach.

I also love growing vigorous climbers through hedges because this doubles up the number of plants in one spot. I simply cut them as part of the hedge. It might mean you can't prune fruiting climbers in the perfect way, but I don't mind because their reduced harvest is made up for the lack of work maintaining them.

Gather

Gather the fruits as they become ripe on the vines – for all three this is when they are slightly soft when given a gentle squeeze.

Eat

Grapes, kiwi and akebias are mainly eaten raw as snacks or for dessert. Akebia flesh is gelatinous and sweet, but you have to spit the hard seeds out. Their thick skins can be stuffed and roasted as a vegetable, like a sweeter potato skin, which is perhaps a more substantial use.

Top right Kiwi berries are the size of grapes and can be eaten whole with the skin; they are hardy and delicious.

Right *Akebia longeracemosa* has particularly long racemes of dusky purple flowers that are a showstopper in spring.

CURRANTS

EFFORT 3/5
TASTINESS 3/5

Ribes rubrum and *Ribes nigrum*

Red, pink and white currants are all various cultivars of the same species *Ribes rubrum* (*rubrum* means 'red'), while blackcurrants are from the closely related species *Ribes nigrum* (*nigrum* means 'black'). Eaten raw, currants can be a little sharp. However, they make good jam, jelly, cordials and additions to cakes where sugar helps balance their flavour. In addition to their excellent nutritional and ornamental value, currants are also tolerant of some shade, making them easy to grow and useful.

NUTRITION:
Fibre (high)
Protein (moderate for redcurrants)
Iron (high)
Potassium (high, for blackcurrants)
Calcium (high, for blackcurrants)
Magnesium (moderate)
Phosphorus (moderate)
Vitamin C (high, especially blackcurrant)
Vitamin E (high, for blackcurrants)
Carotene (moderate, for blackcurrants)
Polyphenols (high)

FAMILY: Grossulariaceae
MAX SIZE: 1.5m high, 1.5m wide
GROW: winter, spring
HARVEST: summer
POT-FRIENDLY: yes (large pot)
SOIL: fertile, free-draining
SITUATION: full sun to partial shade
HARDINESS: H6 (-20°C to -15°C)
ORIGIN: western Europe (*Ribes rubrum*), Europe, Russia and Asia (*Ribes nigrum*)

Grow

Plant bushes 1.5–2m apart in full sun or partial shade at any time of year if planting in a pot, or in winter while dormant if the currant plant is bought bareroot. Alongside gooseberries (see page 86) and raspberries (see page 94), currants can be planted around and below fruit trees (with appropriate spacing), making a useful mid-storey crop in productive plant communities.

Cultivars with RHS Awards of Garden Merit, meaning they were the best under trial, include the blackcurrants 'Big Ben' and 'Ben Hope', the redcurrants 'Jonkheer van Tets' and 'Red Lake', and the white currants 'Blanka' and 'White Grape'.

The main thing to remember with currants is that red, pink and white currants fruit on old wood, while blackcurrants fruit on new wood. This means pruning is slightly different for each category. Ultimately for

Right Blackcurrants crop prolifically in our garden beneath the shade of oak and birch trees.

Opposite Redcurrants' glowing ruby red is a jewel-like addition to gardens as well as useful for jellies.

both, you are aiming for a rough goblet shape with 10 main stems and a slightly open middle for air to flow and light to reach as much of the plant as possible.

To prune, start by removing dead, damaged, diseased or rubbing stems and also low branches hanging close to the ground. Then in winter, while dormant, for blackcurrants simply remove two or three of the oldest stems entirely at ground level and they will grow new shoots from the base in spring.

Red, white and pink currants are pruned at the same time, while dormant in winter, but more lightly. For these, reduce new growth on main branches slightly to restrict size. Remove one or two of the oldest branches completely every year or two to encourage new stems. Prune all small side shoots to two to three buds unless you'd like them to develop into the replacement branches.

You can also grow currants as cordons (trained upright stems) and be more advanced with pruning, but I find my lazy and imperfect approach works really well in plant communities, producing consistently large yields.

Gather

Gather currants when ripe and slightly soft in summer – you can tell when they're ripe, as birds start to eat them. To freeze, clean, dry and remove the stems, then lay the currants in a single layer on a baking tray and freeze. Transfer when solid to an airtight container.

Eat

All currants can be eaten raw, such as with yoghurt or pancakes, or on cakes. Red, white and pink currants can be sweeter if they receive lots of sun. Blackcurrants have a deeper flavour – a little winey and aromatic but still sharp. Personally, I prefer currants in small quantities raw, or cooked to make jam. All currants are rich in nutrients, especially when eaten whole (raw or dried), and filled with antioxidants, but blackcurrants are perhaps the most nutritional.

FIG

EFFORT 2/5
TASTINESS 5/5

Ficus carica

Figs conjure images of holidays in warm climates. However, I live 300m up on the other side of the *Wuthering Heights* moor, a few miles down the road from where Emily Brontë wrote her masterpiece. Our hilltop community is as bleak and storm-battered in winter as you'd imagine and yet one of our neighbours has a fruiting fig tree. It's always worth testing a plant's hardiness for yourself (see page 24).

NUTRITION:
Carbohydrate (moderate)
Fibre (moderate)
Potassium (moderate)
Calcium (moderate)
Magnesium (moderate)
Iron (moderate)
Copper (high)
Manganese (moderate)
Vitamin B6/pyridoxine (moderate)
Polyphenols (high)

FAMILY: Moraceae
MAX SIZE: 2–4m tall, 2–4m wide (if pruned)
GROW: spring
HARVEST: summer
POT-FRIENDLY: yes (large)
SOIL: any
SITUATION: full sun
HARDINESS: H4 (-10°C to -5°C)
ORIGIN: eastern Mediterranean across to Asia

Grow

'Brown Turkey' is a common hardy cultivar and I cannot fault it. Growing exactly as you'd want: beautiful, tropical-looking leaves and delicious brown fruit with sweet, ruby-red flesh. If you live in warmer regions, there are many different cultivars to explore, including variegated 'Panachée' with stripy fruit. 'Hardy Chicago' and 'Rouge de Bordeaux' ripen early, which is good for colder regions. Figs are self-fertile, so you only need one.

In late summer to early autumn, remove any large fruits that are still hard and green, as these won't ripen. Leave only pea-sized fruitlets to crop next summer. These baby figs begin growing in summer, overwintering as small fruitlets that ripen the next season. In very cold regions you may need to protect these fruitlets by stuffing dried plant material like straw or meadow clippings around them.

Although 'Brown Turkey' is hardy, it will fruit better with a helping hand. Plant figs in your sunniest sheltered spot protected from wind by hedges, a wall or fence. This will create a warming microclimate to encourage ripening while protecting fruitlets in winter.

Fig trees want to be huge and it helps to encourage fruiting instead of foliage by restricting their roots. Dig a large square pit, 60 × 60 × 60cm, then line the sides with cheap patio slabs or submerge a large terracotta pot. Refill with soil and plant the fig tree into this.

Left When ripe, figs have rich and soft ruby flesh that is packed with natural sugars.

Roots will grow out of the bottom but will be restrained, and the plant will want to fruit rather than produce lots of lush growth.

Pruning will also help restrict the size of your fig tree to keep it manageable. Figs fruit on shoot tips, making it better to take out a few large branches each year when they grow too large, leaving a stump about 10–15cm long from which new shoots will grow. Figs can also be trained in a fan shape against walls.

Gather

Figs are ripe when deep brown and slightly squidgy; they may even be a little sticky. They will pull away from the tree easily at this stage. Figs can be stored in the fridge for a few weeks or dried in a dehydrator, either whole or cut into halves or quarters. Once dried, keep in an airtight container in a cool, dark cupboard for up to a year.

Eat

Rich in carbohydrates in the form of natural sugars and lots of dietary fibre, figs are one of the best natural sweet snacks you can eat. They remain my closest healthy alternative to chocolate and sweets, and they grow for free. Aren't perennial edibles brilliant!

Top right 'Brown Turkey' may be a common cultivar in areas with cold winters but it does everything you want from a delicious fig!

Right Milder areas may grow many exciting cultivars of various sizes, flavours and colours, including stripy 'Panachée'.

GOOSEBERRY

EFFORT ●●○○○
TASTINESS ●●●●●

Ribes uva-crispa

I remember a gooseberry bush growing in our garden as a child. No one ever did anything to it, and still it fruited each year. Gooseberries are that easy to grow. Unfortunately, many used for cooking are tart or sour until baked, which put me off for years.

NUTRITION:
Carbohydrate (moderate)
Fibre (high)
Potassium (high)
Magnesium (moderate)
Calcium (moderate)
Phosphorus (moderate)
Vitamin C (high)
Beta-carotene (moderate)
Polyphenols (high)
Phytosterols (low-moderate)

FAMILY: Grossulariaceae
MAX SIZE: 1.5m tall, 1.5m wide
GROW: winter, spring
HARVEST: mid-summer
POT-FRIENDLY: no
SOIL: any
SITUATION: full sun to partial shade
HARDINESS: H6 (-20°C to -15°C)
ORIGIN: mainland Europe, North Africa and Middle East

That is, until my gooseberry world was turned on its head when I tasted one of the dessert types that are ready to eat raw, which taste as sweet as the best grape. It's the sweet dessert cultivars I want to focus on.

Grow

Gooseberries are as hardy as anything and tolerant of shade, making them one of my go-to plants for forage gardening. Space bushes 1.5m apart.

There are many good cultivars out there to choose from, but if you want sweet, it's important you choose carefully. 'Leveller' is a reliable yellow-green cultivar with large, sweet fruits. 'Martlet' and 'Whinham's Industry' both have large, sweet, red fruits, the latter being particularly good on heavy soil and in partial shade, useful for growing under fruit or nut trees.

There is lots of technical pruning advice out there, but I've personally had the best results by letting gooseberry bushes grow large and unruly and only pruning out the oldest or damaged stems every now and then while the bush is dormant in winter. It can be worth removing low-hanging branches to make it easier to reach in and pick in the summer.

It's possible to propagate more gooseberry bushes by taking hardwood cuttings while the plants are dormant in winter. Cut a 20cm length of young woody stem, trimming just beneath some leaf buds. Plant the lower half or two-thirds into soil or three

Left A bounty of super sweet dessert gooseberries picked in their prime.

to five cuttings per 2-litre pot of compost, then leave somewhere outside until spring, when the cuttings should root and start growing.

Gather

Pick gooseberries by hand as you need them when they turn soft, giving them a gentle squeeze. Taste test to check they are as sweet as they can be. They will ripen steadily over a few weeks on the plants.

Above Gooseberries can be quite large and are ripe when slightly squidgy to the touch, taste one if unsure.

Right They are among our most prolific crops, quite a feat considering I do nothing to look after ours!

Eat

Sweet gooseberries can be eaten raw like grapes and to me they taste just as delicious. Add them to yoghurt, dessert or breakfast for a nutritional boost. Alternatively, make into jams or fools, or add to cakes and tarts. Gooseberries can be frozen whole for later use in cooking.

Like many fruits, since gooseberries are low in calories they make a healthy alternative to sweets and chocolate, with the bonus of being high in antioxidants and vitamin C.

LEMON

EFFORT 2/5
TASTINESS 4/5

Citrus × limon 'Four Seasons'

Before I changed careers to run my landscape design studio, I did my fair share of time in open-plan offices where my colleagues and I grew as many plants as we could before HR told us off. It was here I witnessed with my own eyes the magic of lemons appearing on an evergreen pot plant year after year.

NUTRITION:
Fibre (moderate, in peel)
Potassium (high)
Iron (moderate)
Copper (moderate)
Zinc (moderate)
Vitamin B6/pyridoxine (moderate)
Vitamin C (high)
Carotene (moderate)
Flavonoids (high, in peel)

FAMILY: Rutaceae
MAX SIZE: 4m tall, 1.5m wide (smaller in pots)
GROW: year round
HARVEST: all year
POT-FRIENDLY: yes, using citrus/ericaceous compost in pots 30–45cm-plus
SOIL: acidic, neutral
SITUATION: full sun
HARDINESS: H2 (1°C to 5°C)
ORIGIN: cultigen suspected to come from eastern India

Left In a very sunny south-facing window, small lemon trees can fruit all year round.

Opposite While you might not grow all the lemons you need, one tree can produce a steady supply and smells beautiful.

Lemons are a complex hybrid cultivar of three citrus species: *Citrus maxima*, *C. medica* and *C. reticulata* which originate from different parts of south and east Asia, especially the Himalaya, South East Asia and China. Although frost tender (vulnerable when temperatures dip below 1–5°C), they can be grown in colder climates indoors during winter.

Grow

In this book I'm highlighting the lemon cultivar 'Four Seasons' as a flavoursome crop that's easy to grow indoors in pots. There are other small cultivars, such as 'Meyers', but 'Four Seasons' is widely regarded as very reliable.

The most important conditions to note for growing lemons is that they need every second of direct sunlight you can give and they must be grown in acidic or neutral soil because lemon trees are intolerant of alkaline conditions. Lemons, like all citrus plants, are not hardy, so they must be grown inside on a sunny, south-facing window or in a heated greenhouse or conservatory in winter. Of course, if you live in warmer regions with temperatures staying about 1°C, then lemons will thrive outdoors.

If you have a heated greenhouse or conservatory and can plant the lemon tree in the ground, it will be very happy as long as the soil is acidic or neutral. For most of us, lemons are grown in large containers with specialist citrus compost (or ericaceous). Water must also not be alkaline, so if you live in a hard-water area where limescale builds up, you must use rainwater or distilled water. Feed with a liquid citrus specialist fertiliser in spring and summer.

When grown indoors in pots, unless you have a super-sunny, south-facing window, for best plant health and cropping move your lemon tree outside in spring and summer when temperatures (especially at night) are above 5°C. Over the years, repot into slightly larger containers, gently scraping off loose old compost so you can add more fresh compost.

Pinch back the tips of new shoots in summer to encourage bushiness and restrict size.

Gather

When fruit is ripe it will lift away from the plant. If it doesn't, leave until ripe – lemons do not continue ripening off the plant.

Eat

Use lemon in drinks, cakes and to drizzle on salads and other dishes. It is worth noting that the rind and flesh contain the dietary fibre and flavonoids, and the juice has significantly less. Find ways to include peel and zest in your diet to benefit.

MULBERRY

EFFORT
TASTINESS

Morus nigra and *Morus alba*

A less known perennial edible is *Morus nigra*, the black mulberry from Iran, which produces lots of delicious fruit in late summer. The fruits look like large, black raspberries or blackberries and taste fairly similar, perhaps a tad sharper. Rarely sold in shops because they don't store well, they are a gardener's treat. The white mulberry from China, *Morus alba*, does produce pale fruit but is mainly grown for its leaves which are eaten as a cooked green.

NUTRITION:

Fruit
Natural sugars (high)
Fibre (moderate)
Iron (moderate)
Vitamin C (high)
Polyphenol
– anthocyanins (high)

Leaves
Fibre (moderate)
Protein (high, for a cooked green)
Calcium (high)
Iron (high)
Polyphenols (high)

FAMILY: Moraceae
MAX SIZE: 8m tall, 8m wide
GROW: winter (bareroot), spring (pot-grown)
HARVEST: late summer
POT-FRIENDLY: no (except specific cultivars)
SOIL: any free-draining
SITUATION: full sun
HARDINESS: H6 (-20°C to -15°C)
ORIGIN: Iran (*Morus nigra*), Central China (*Morus alba*)

Grow

One of the best black mulberries for yield and flavour in cooler climates is 'Illinois Everbearing', which will fruit over a number of weeks in late summer. Plant mulberry in a sunny spot, providing lots of room because it will grow into a reasonably large tree over 8m wide and tall – not one for a small garden, but useful in parks or community gardens. Alternatively, there is a short cultivar called 'Matsunaga', sold as 'Mojo Berry', which grows to 1.5m tall and almost as wide. This can be grown in large pots.

White mulberry is also large, but it can be pollarded (cutting the top off) at about 1–1.5m once its trunk is at least 7–10cm in diameter. This may sound brutal at first, but it will encourage lots of new shoots for young tender leaves at picking height. Every other year remove a few of the older branches to encourage fresh growth, which also contains the mulberry's size. Like lime tree (see page 60), this means it can be grown in a low plant community without overly shading everything else. Position the mulberry carefully at the back of a plant community, so the front plants receive maximum sunlight.

Above White mulberry, *Morus alba*, is grown for its edible leaves, though the berries have a mild and sweet flavour too.

Gather

In late summer, when ripe, mulberries can be picked from lower branches or the tree shaken for ripe fruit to drop. You can lay a sheet or large towel out to help gather the fallen fruit. They can stain your hands, so you might want to wear gloves. To gather leaves on white mulberry, simply pick the younger, fresher looking ones as needed. These can be stored in an airtight bag or container in the fridge for a few days.

Above Black mulberry, *Morus nigra*, produces an absolutely enormous quantity of delicious berries in summer. They don't store very well in shops, making them a grower's secret.

Eat

Black mulberries don't store well and are best eaten within a day. They can be used in desserts such as pies, in syrups and even to make mulberry wine. They are rich in anthocyanins, powerful antioxidants that help our bodies resist a number of diseases.

The leaves of white mulberry need to be steamed for a few minutes, boiled lightly or cooked within a dish to make them more palatable. They are very rich in nutrients for a cooked green and comparable to spinach, with good amounts of protein, iron, calcium and various polyphenols.

PEARS

EFFORT
TASTINESS

Pyrus communis and *Pyrus pyrifolia*

Sweet and succulent pears are a healthy dessert and grow on perennial trees. I grow two species of pear: the common pear (*Pyrus communis*), which originates from Europe to the Middle East, and the nashi pear (*Pyrus pyrifolia*) from China.

NUTRITION:
Fibre (moderate)
Potassium (low-moderate)
Copper (moderate)
Vitamin K (moderate)
Polyphenols (high)

FAMILY: Rosaceae
MAX SIZE: 4m tall, 4m wide
GROW: winter, spring
HARVEST: autumn
POT-FRIENDLY: no
SOIL: any
SITUATION: full sun
HARDINESS: H6 (-20°C to -15°C)
ORIGIN: mainland Europe to western Middle East (*Pyrus communis*), China (*Pyrus pyrifolia*)

Less known in the West, nashi pears are golden spheres, which look like a russet apple. Grown in the same way as the common pear, nashi pears have a firm, grainy texture and a flavour somewhere between pear, melon and strawberry.

Grow

There are many cultivars of both common and nashi pear, and like apples (page 74) it is best to taste test some grown locally. Discover your favourites in nearby orchards or farms, or contact other growers who can advise on cultivars suitable for your garden's conditions and your flavour preferences.

I've found reliable cultivars include the common pear 'Beurré Hardy' and the tried-and-tested 'Conference', as well as the nashi pear 'Shinseiki'. These have all grown well for me in drier southern England, as well as on our farm in Yorkshire (H4/-10°C to -5°C).

Pears are grown on quince rootstocks, offering different levels of vigour and size. Quince A rootstock can grow up to 4m tall and wide; Quince C reaches 3m tall and wide. The latter is

Left Pears make an excellent addition to cakes and other baked products, in addition to being eaten raw.

Opposite A relatively young pear 'Concorde' growing happily in the area our chickens free roam; it's full sun here but also extremely windswept.

probably the best option for most gardens. Order bareroot pears in winter when they are dormant. These will arrive without soil and should be planted right away to the soil mark beneath the graft join.

Space pear trees just a little wider than their final width – for instance, plant Quince C pear trees 3–3.5m apart, giving both canopies plenty of room and light. To maximise the use of space in an orchard or plant community containing multiple fruit and nut trees, space them in a zigzag grid, essentially forming triangles between them.

If you plan to grow lots of sun- or partial-shade-loving perennial edibles beneath pear trees, it is worth spacing them further apart to allow more light through when they are fully grown.

Gather

Ripe pears lift away easily from the tree. For some late cultivars, like 'Beurré Hardy', it may be necessary to pick the fruit unripe just before frosts start. They will ripen in storage. Store pears carefully in trays, ensuring they don't touch one another as this can encourage rot.

Eat

The skin of pears contains the most polyphenols and dietary fibre, making it well worth eating. Polyphenols are antioxidants and can help reduce blood pressure and inflammation when eaten regularly. Recent research has also shown pears contain some beneficial compounds unique to this fruit.

RASPBERRY

EFFORT 1/5
TASTINESS 5/5

Rubus idaeus

My favourite raspberries are the autumn-fruiting cultivars from the species *Rubus idaeus*, which I want to focus on. They are incredibly easy to grow and put up with competition from smaller plants growing at their base, making them useful for edible plant communities.

NUTRITION:
Fibre (high)
Manganese (high)
Magnesium (moderate)
Phosphorus (moderate)
Iron (moderate)
Vitamin B6/pyridoxine (moderate)
Vitamin B7/biotin (moderate)
Vitamin B9/folate (high)
Vitamin C (high)
Vitamin E (moderate)
Polyphenols (high)
Phytosterols (moderate)

FAMILY: Rosaceae
MAX SIZE: 1.5m tall, 60cm wide
GROW: winter, spring
HARVEST: autumn
POT-FRIENDLY: no
SOIL: any
SITUATION: full sun to partial shade
HARDINESS: H6 (-20°C to -15°C)
ORIGIN: entire temperate Northern Hemisphere

Cropping occurs gradually over two to three months from late summer onward, perfect for regular fresh picking over a long period. Importantly, raspberries are delicious, as good as any sweets. If you have space, you can grow summer-fruiting raspberries too for a large one-off crop in mid-summer. But I think autumn raspberries are where it's at.

Grow

Order raspberries as bareroot plants while dormant in winter and plant as soon as you receive them, 50cm apart and allowing 1.8m between rows/groups. You can also buy raspberry plants in pots all year round, but these will be more expensive. If you already have some raspberries, or someone you know does, dig out clumps of roots in winter and move them to your garden for free.

With autumn-fruiting raspberries, all you have to remember is to cut them to the ground in winter while dormant. New shoots will emerge in spring which will fruit that summer. They are also self-supporting, with no need for support structures.

My tried-and-tested favourites are red 'Joan J' (thornless) or 'Polka' and yellow 'All Gold'. Vigorous growers, they will happily grow through other plants and slowly spread around the garden.

Summer-fruiting raspberries do need support and it's important in winter to cut out two-year-old canes which fruited that summer, leaving the new canes to fruit the following year.

Left 'All Gold' and 'Polka' are two of my all-time favourite plants to grow, they taste utterly delicious.

Above 'Joan J' has few to no spines on the stems. It is slightly less vigorous than 'Polka'.

Above 'All Gold' brings a beautiful golden colour to gardens and tastes as lovely as the red cultivars.

Gather

As fruits ripen, gently tug downward and they will come away easily when ready. If they don't, leave them another day or two. Place the raspberries in a container gently because they damage easily. Alternatively, you can pop them in a sealed bag or airtight container and store in the freezer for up to a year.

Eat

Raspberries can be eaten fresh as a dessert, which is my preferred use both for ease and taste. Try them with yoghurt and a sprinkling of homemade elderflower cordial (see page 148). Even better, eat directly from the plant, as I tend to do… Of course, raspberries can be cooked in pies or turned into a coulis to pour on desserts or for use in drinks.

RHUBARB

EFFORT
TASTINESS

Rheum × hybridum

Rhubarb is the crop I recommend every new food grower starts with because it's so easy! If you have space, you need never pay for rhubarb again. Being a starter perennial edible doesn't diminish the fact that rhubarb is a delicious and versatile crop, especially when you start exploring the many different cultivars available today.

NUTRITION:
Fibre (moderate)
Potassium (moderate)
Calcium (low)
Manganese (moderate)
Vitamin C (moderate)
Vitamin K (high)
Polyphenols (moderate)

FAMILY: Polygonaceae
MAX SIZE: 70cm tall, 90cm wide
GROW: autumn, spring
HARVEST: spring, summer
POT-FRIENDLY: yes (large)
SOIL: any water-retentive
SITUATION: full sun to partial shade
HARDINESS: H5 (-15°C to -10°C)
ORIGIN: hybrid cross between *Rheum palmatum* from China to Vietnam and *Rheum rhaponticum* from Bulgaria

Botanically rhubarb is considered a vegetable because we eat the petiole (the stem of the leaf); in botany a fruit forms from the ovary or associated parts of a flower. When it comes to consumption, however, rhubarb is categorised as a fruit because of the way we eat it.

Grow

Buy rhubarb plants in pots all year round or bareroot (that is, with no pot or compost) in winter when dormant. Plant so that the roots are buried and the crown – the growing point – is at soil level but not covered. Space plants 90cm apart.

In addition to normal growing, rhubarb can be forced for sweeter stems. Forcing is when the dormant crown is covered with a specialist upturned pot or large bucket at the end of winter to exclude all light, forcing the new shoots to stretch upwards, searching for light. This results in delicious, bright pink-red stems. Only force the first batch of stems and rotate

Left 'Canada Red' maintains its deep red colour all summer but it's particularly red in spring.

Opposite I bought three rhubarb plants when we moved to our garden and I've since divided them all to produce lots more plants for free, significantly increasing the size of our patch.

the plants you cover to give them one year off between forcing.

There are loads of cultivars of rhubarb available, including the classics 'Timperley Early' and 'Victoria', which are both delicious. I grow cultivars with red stems through most of the season because I like the colour, though green stems are perfectly edible and have lots of flavour.

'Champagne' is an early-growing cultivar that's perfect for forcing; 'Canada Red' has small, very red, sweet stems; and 'Raspberry Red' has delicious thicker stems. Rhubarb is particularly useful in edible plant communities as a very large ground cover. It needs full sun but is tolerant of some shade. Rhubarb will go dormant if it's too dry in the summer.

Gather

Pick stems at least 30–40cm long, taking from the outside of the plant first. Snap sideways and they'll pull away easily; this is better than cutting, as the cut can rot. Always keep 30 per cent of the leaves on the plant at a time for photosynthesis. Cut off and discard the leaf as this is poisonous.

Eat

Chop rhubarb stems into 2–3cm chunks, place in an oven dish with a little sugar to taste, cover with foil and roast for 15 minutes at 200°C (fan oven). Remove the foil, stir and cook for a final 5 minutes. An alternative to sugar is to coat the rhubarb in the juice of an orange and a good handful of chopped sweet cicely leaves (see page 120).

Rhubarb isn't the most nutritional of plants, but it is quite rich in potassium and vitamin K, plus it contributes to vitamin C intake. It has enough polyphenols to make it a contributor to antioxidants, helping reduce inflammation. A curiosity is that rhubarb contains very high amounts of calcium but this is locked up in oxalic acid – giving its sharpness – making it hard for our bodies to absorb.

STRAWBERRY

EFFORT (2 of 5)
TASTINESS (5 of 5)

Fragaria × ananassa

The strawberries we buy in shops are a hybrid between *Fragaria chiloensis* from Bolivia and Chile (as well as further north into California and British Columbia) and *Fragaria virginiana* subsp. *virginiana* from North America. They are one of those crops where the flavour difference between shop-bought fruits and homegrown is huge. Picked from a plant warmed in the sun, the fruit is much, much sweeter and tastier. If you're a bit underwhelmed by shop-bought strawberries, please give them another chance by growing your own plants.

NUTRITION:
Fibre (high)
Potassium (moderate)
Manganese (moderate)
Vitamin B9/folate (moderate)
Vitamin C (high)
Polyphenols (high)

FAMILY: Rosaceae
MAX SIZE: 30cm tall, 30cm wide
GROW: spring, summer, autumn
HARVEST: summer

POT-FRIENDLY: yes
SOIL: any
SITUATION: full sun to dappled shade
HARDINESS: H6 (-20°C to -15°C)
ORIGIN: Bolivia, Chile, and West Coast USA and Canada (*Fragaria chiloensis*), eastern Canada, USA and Mexico (*Fragaria virginiana* subsp. *virginiana*)

Grow

Cultivar choice has the biggest impact on flavour and nutrition. 'Honeyoye' (fruits early summer) and 'Cambridge Favourite' (fruits mid-summer) are two of my favourites for vigour and taste. Both come with an RHS Award of Garden Merit, as do many others, including 'Pegasus' and 'Rhapsody' (both fruit late summer). There are so many strawberry cultivars that it's worth growing a few to try for yourself in the first year, then propagate more of your favourites for free the following year.

Propagating strawberries is as easy as eating them. After they fruit in the summer they send out long shoots called runners, or botanically stolons. These stems stretch away from the main plant before new plants form along them at intervals. All you have to do is wait for these young plants to root, then you can either leave them to grow or move them to a new position or pot. These are genetic clones of the parent plant, giving you more of your favourite cultivar for free!

Plant strawberries 45cm apart to create patches of edible ground cover. They need full sun to fruit best but will still crop in partial shade, making them useful to grow around and below bigger plants in an edible plant community, such as beneath fruit bushes or rhubarb.

Right 'Cambridge Favourite' may be a common cultivar but it remains one of the most vigorous and delicious for me.

Opposite Homegrown strawberries in summer taste phenomenal compared to shop bought.

Gather

Pick strawberries as they turn red, signalling they are ripe. Some cultivars ripen all at once over a few weeks, while others such as 'Finesse' produce smaller fruit over a number of summer months. Birds and other wildlife love them too, so make sure you beat them to it!

Eat

Strawberries are amazing because they contain low levels of natural sugar but are still extremely sweet, making them a very healthy sweet treat. They're high in dietary fibre and a handful contains more vitamin C than an orange, alongside many other vitamins and minerals that contribute to our daily nutrition. Packed with polyphenols, strawberries are thought to help reduce inflammation, so, if eaten regularly in our diet, contribute to reducing chronic illness. This strengthens the argument that humanity should invest more time in cultivating sweet but healthy fruits to heal rather than inventing new unhealthy snacks that harm...

OTHER PERENNIAL FRUIT WORTH A TRY

- Blueberries *Vaccinium* spp.
- Cherries *Prunus* spp.
- Chilean guava *Ugni molinae*
- Damson *Prunus insititia*
- Flowering dogwood *Cornus kousa*
- Honeyberry *Lonicera caerulea*
- Green gage *Prunus domestica*
- Japanese rose *Rosa rugosa*
- Loganberry *Rubus × loganobaccus*
- Medlar *Mespilus germanica*
- Passionfruit *Passiflora caerula*
- Pineapple guava *Feijoa sellowiana*
- Plums *Prunus domestica*
- Quince *Cydonia oblonga*
- Sloe *Prunus spinosa*
- Tayberry *Rubus fruiticosus × idaeus*

Herbs

Herbs are such romantic plants and incredible sources of pollen and nectar for pollinators. Easy to grow, needing almost no care once established, herbs have a wide tolerance of climates, from damp to dry. I often include herbs in garden designs purely for these reasons, with their edibility a bonus. Once a herb bed is established, you need never buy those herbs again, saving you money and reducing packaging.

Nutrition: I've discovered that herbs are among the most nutritionally dense plants we can eat. They are only eaten in small quantities, so by adding some to as many meals as possible you can increase your plant intake, supplementing nutrition to improve health over time.

Left Edible herbs are as delicious as they are gorgeous, with soft, silvery foliage set against brightly coloured flowers, as on curry plant (left), *Helichrysum italicum*, and white flowered lavender (right) *Lavandula* × *intermedia* 'Edelweiss'.

BAY TREE

EFFORT
TASTINESS

Laurus nobilis

Bay leaves are nutrient-dense, but we tend to eat only very small portions as a spice to flavour dishes. The leathery evergreen leaves are added whole during cooking to infuse the dish with their flavour and nutrients, then removed before serving because they're tough and hard to chew.

NUTRITION:
Carbohydrate (moderate)
Protein (moderate)
Iron (exceptionally high)
Calcium (very high)
Manganese (very high)
Potassium (high)
Magnesium (high)
Zinc (moderate)
Copper (moderate)
Phosphorus (moderate)
Provitamin A (moderate)

FAMILY: Lauraceae
MAX SIZE: 10m tall, 8m wide
GROW: spring
HARVEST: year round
POT-FRIENDLY: yes, large pots 45cm-plus
SOIL: any free-draining
SITUATION: full sun to partial shade
HARDINESS: H4 (-10°C to -5°C)
ORIGIN: Mediterranean

When ground into a powder, bay leaves (fresh or dry) can be added more safely to dishes, making them more digestible. In low quantities, if used regularly, bay is a beneficial part of our diet.

Grow

Grow bay trees in a large pot or in the ground. They are more tolerant of the cold if their roots are in the ground rather than exposed in a pot and develop thicker, woodier stems as they age. Said to be hardy to -5°C, I have found bay can withstand far lower temperatures down to -10°C, even in the very wet and exposed climate of our hilltop garden in Yorkshire, reminding us that it's always good to experiment with hardiness to check plant tolerances for ourselves.

A sunny spot helps protect from cold, though in my experience shelter is more important for bay, which can grow well in partial shade. Buildings, fences, hedges and other large evergreen plants can help create a protective microclimate.

Bay is very happy to be pruned and cut back, with new growth emerging from trunks and branches just beneath cuts. This allows you to restrict bay to a certain size if grown in a pot or small garden. Pruning does remove significant energy from the plant, however, so aim to cut back only a third of the plant every year or two at most.

Left Bay leaves can be dried by spreading them on a plate or tray on a sunny windowsill for a couple of weeks.

Opposite Grow a bay tree and you need never buy this herb ever again, nor your friends, family or neighbours!

Gather

Pick bay leaves as you need them – they come away easily with a little tug. You can use the leaves fresh or dry them for later use. To dry bay leaves, lay them on a piece of baking parchment on a tray next to a sunny window in a warm, dry room. They will dry themselves over a couple of weeks. Use a dehydrator for faster results.

Once dry, store the dried leaves whole or grind them into a fine powder using a pestle and mortar. If powdered, remove any remaining stems. Flavour and nutrients are better preserved in whole leaves, so you might want to store whole dried leaves and grind as needed later. Store the whole or ground bay in an airtight container somewhere cool and dark. Replace every six months to maintain the highest levels of nutrients and flavour, though bay will remain usable for much longer.

Eat

Add one to three whole bay leaves, fresh or dry, to infuse flavour into dishes, remembering to remove them before serving as people can choke on them. Use whole leaves in stews, casseroles, pasta sauces and preserves where the leaves have time to infuse.

Alternatively, add ⅛–¼ teaspoon of ground bay to seasoning mixes for use on vegetables or meat, and in breads, stuffings and sausages. Ground bay is more potent and stays in the dish, so meals need less of it.

Try a side-by-side comparison of the same dish with whole leaf or ground bay to help you understand the different flavour effects.

CHIVES

EFFORT
TASTINESS

Allium schoenoprasum

Chives are one of those foolproof plants that every single person should be growing. No one in the temperate world should be wasting money on chives! Small and indestructible, with pretty, narrow, grass-like leaves and pale mauve flowers in spring and summer, chives are also used by bees and other pollinators. Dot them through your garden in challenging corners or between bigger plants for welcome colour, food and wildlife support.

NUTRITION:
Protein (moderate)
Calcium (high)
Potassium (high)
Iron (high)
Vitamin C (high)
Carotene (high)
Phytosterol (moderate)
Vitamin K (high)
Folate (moderate)

FAMILY: Amaryllidaceae
MAX SIZE: 40cm tall, 40cm wide
GROW: year round
HARVEST: spring, summer, autumn
POT-FRIENDLY: yes
SOIL: any free-draining
SITUATION: full sun to partial shade
HARDINESS: H6 (-20°C to -15°C)
ORIGIN: temperate Northern Hemisphere

Grow

If you aren't already growing chives and take one thing from this book, please make it a promise that you'll plant some. Chives are small bulbous plants that are very tolerant of abuse. Grow in full sun or partial shade, in dry fertile soil or rich heavy soil, in exposed spots or in a pot, with heavy competition – you name it, chives will find a way.

Chives are the ultimate plant-and-forget herb. I literally dig a hole, plant chives to the depth they were before, or to the compost level if pot-grown, give them a glug of water and leave them to get on with it. I've never had chives die on me; they've always grown vigorously, multiplying bulbs and therefore leaves with each year.

You can grow chives from seed, but the easiest method is to simply replant chive plants. Someone you know will have some; ask them if you can dig out a handful of bulbs with roots and leaves. Replant in your garden as one small clump or divide further and plant multiple plants – just one bulb with roots and shoots is enough.

For container life, start chives in a 20cm pot of compost and in a few years, when the clump expands to fill the pot, you can either plant into a bigger 30cm pot or divide the clump into quarters and replant one quarter. Chives in pots will produce healthy leaf growth if they never dry out completely and are given a liquid fertiliser every few weeks (not necessary in the ground).

By growing some chives in a pot, you can bring them inside for fresh pickings over winter, while those outside in the cold will go dormant. They won't survive forever indoors as they prefer the cold, but it's a handy trick.

Opposite Chives offer a welcome splash of colour in gardens, especially when dotted through the garden.

Above Loved by pollinators, the entire plant is also edible from the leaves, flowers and flower buds.

Gather

I snip off leaves and flowers I need for meals with scissors as required. Or, if I'm feeling cavalier, I pull them off by hand. I'm a rebel. New leaves will soon regrow anyway.

Eat

Chive leaves and flowers can be eaten raw. I snip them directly into meals or as a garnish. I love them in mashed potato, potato salad, ramen, stir-fries, omelettes, sandwiches and soups, as well as sprinkled liberally on almost everything as a garnish.

As with other onion family plants, the green leaves of chives are proportionately rich in minerals and protein. Obviously, we only eat small amounts of chives at any one time, which limits our nutritional intake, but by growing our own we can eat generous quantities and often. A nifty nutrient boost.

FENNEL

Foeniculum vulgare

EFFORT
TASTINESS

Fennel is a nutritious and super-stylish plant used by garden designers the world over. Given it grows with ease everywhere, there is absolutely no reason for anyone to buy fennel leaves or seeds.

NUTRITION:
Carbohydrate (moderate)
Protein (high in seeds)
Calcium (high)
Potassium (high)
Magnesium (high)
Iron (high)
B-vitamins (moderate)
Vitamin C (high in fresh leaves)
Polyphenols (high)

FAMILY: Apiaceae
MAX SIZE: 2m tall, 50cm wide
GROW: spring
HARVEST: spring, summer
POT-FRIENDLY: no
SOIL: any
SITUATION: full sun
HARDINESS: H5 (-15°C to -10°C)
ORIGIN: Mediterranean to Ethiopia and Nepal

Outside of its natural range fennel can be problematic in the wild as an invasive plant, but it's easily controlled in gardens by eating all the seeds, thus preventing its spread. And when you find out how good those seeds are for you, there's no way you'd let even one escape.

Grow

Fennel needs full direct sunlight to grow well and struggles if surrounded by large, shade-creating plants. It will grow in sandy and gravelly, free-draining soil, but I have always found it more vigorous in fertile, moisture-retentive soil, though still free-draining.

Sow seeds 1cm deep in pots or directly in the ground in spring and water gently. Cover pots with a transparent lid to lock in humidity and warmth until the seeds germinate. Then grow the seedlings to a size large enough to plant out, with about four to six adult leaves.

The straight species *Foeniculum vulgare* has green leaves, while *Foeniculum vulgare* var. *purpureum*, known as bronze fennel, has slightly purple-bronze stems and leaves. Depending on where you source bronze fennel,

Left Fennel seeds are edible and taste very sweet if eaten green.

Opposite Valued by garden designers for its fluffy leaves, fennel is a stylish edible perennial.

it can be a very dark shade. I have always found the green plants the most vigorous.

Fennel bulbs are produced by cultivars of a very distinct variety called Florence fennel (*Foeniculum vulgare* var. *azoricum*). Not true bulbs, these are swollen leaf petioles just above ground. Otherwise, the leaves, flowers and seeds can all be used in the same way. Eating the bulb, the base of the plant, will kill it – goodbye perennial. To maintain fennel as a perennial for leaves and seeds, it's better to grow the species or bronze fennel.

Fresh green leaves contain very high quantities of vitamin C (not in dried seeds), carotenoids, folates (B-vitamins) and minerals. This is similar but more condensed than the bulbs of Florence fennel. However, we eat smaller quantities of fennel leaves, so overall it probably balances out. Like most herbs, a few fennel leaves chopped into meals regularly is beneficial to our diets.

Gather

Snip leaves off as you need them, concentrating on the fine pieces rather than thicker stems. Seeds can be eaten green direct from the plant as they swell, and these are a sweet and delicious treat. Alternatively, wait until the seeds begin to dry on the plant, then snip off the entire seed head and place upside down in a paper bag. Leave somewhere dry and the seeds will eventually fall or can be shaken off. These can then be stored in an airtight container.

Eat

Dried seeds are either ground to a powder and added to dishes or used whole in the likes of bread, cakes and biscuits. Dried fennel seeds are highly nutritious, rich in minerals and with as much protein as legumes, making them useful in diets as a spice. Seeds can also be steeped in boiling water to make refreshing fennel tea but only a small fraction of the nutrition is transferred to the water.

LAVENDER

EFFORT 1/5
TASTINESS 5/5

Lavandula × intermedia

Lavender is one of the few perennial edibles in this book where you probably won't receive much beneficial nutrition from it, as it's more about flavour. The flowers of all lavenders are edible and used to add a floral flavour to drinks, ice cream and other desserts. And it makes a beautiful addition to the garden in summer, humming with bees, hoverflies and butterflies during the hottest months.

NUTRITION:
Unlikely to be consumed in any meaningful amount.
Polyphenols
Phytosterols

FAMILY: Lamiaceae
MAX SIZE: 80cm tall, 80cm wide
GROW: spring, summer
HARVEST: summer
POT-FRIENDLY: yes
SOIL: any free-draining
SITUATION: full sun
HARDINESS: H5 (-15°C to -10°C)
ORIGIN: France and Spain

Grow

I imagine summer fragrance and airiness when I think of lavender, but it's a tough plant if grown in full sun and free-draining soil. Drought tolerant and needing few nutrients in the soil to grow well, it can also tolerate cold, wet winters. This tolerance of various conditions is the reason for its popularity in gardens.

There are many species and cultivars of lavender and my favourites are of the *Lavandula* × *intermedia* hybrid. These have been among the most reliable for me, with prolific numbers of beautiful flowers held on long, delicate stems. 'Edelweiss' has large, grey-white flowers, while 'Sussex' has the traditional blue, and both taste the same to me. Taste some different varieties yourself to see if you have a favourite.

Grow from cuttings in mid-summer by taking 10cm stems without flowers, stripping the lower two-thirds of leaves without damaging the stem. Plant three to five cuttings to just below the leaves in a 7–9cm pot of compost and cover with a transparent lid until rooted in a month or so. Keep the compost

Right The flowers of lavender can be added to cakes and drinks for flavouring.

slightly moist and out of direct sunlight until roots form and leaves are actively growing again.

After flowering, trim off all flower stems down to the leaves to let more light reach them, giving them enough time to grow and toughen up ahead of winter.

Above left *Lavandula* × *intermedia* 'Edelweiss' is a robust and vigorous cultivar with a large number of white flowers in summer.

Above right *Lavandula* × *intermedia* 'Sussex' is another beautiful, prolific cultivar with classic lavender blue flowers.

Gather

Pick flower stems as needed. They're best dried for storage and later use. Lay them on a tray on a warm, sunny windowsill for a few weeks or use a dehydrator.

Eat

Once dried, crumble the tiny, individual flowers from each flower stem, without damaging them too much, to loosen them from the stem onto a plate. They can then be stored or used in dishes. Add lavender flowers to ice cream, meringue, bread, cakes, cordials and syrups. Use whole flower-heads with the stem trimmed off to garnish cakes and drinks.

LOVAGE

EFFORT
TASTINESS

Levisticum officinale

Umami is a recently described flavour that means a lingering savoury taste, sitting alongside sweet, sour, salty and bitter. Lovage primarily tastes like its relatives, celery and parsley, as a result of its aromatic chemicals phthalides.

NUTRITION: Despite limited credible data, it is considered nutrient-dense and known to contain polyphenols, vitamin E, potassium, calcium, magnesium and iron.

FAMILY: Apiaceae
MAX SIZE: 2.5m tall, 1m wide
GROW: spring
HARVEST: spring, summer, autumn
POT-FRIENDLY: no
SOIL: any
SITUATION: full sun
HARDINESS: H6 (-20°C to -15°C)
ORIGIN: Iran and Afghanistan

These phthalides combine with high levels of glutamic and aspartic acids and lovage's naturally high levels of potassium salts to produce the lingering umami taste. To me it tastes brothy, and that's exactly why lovage is traditionally used.

Grow

Sow seeds in spring into individual 10cm pots of compost, covering lightly with a thin dusting of compost. Water gently, cover with a transparent lid and place somewhere sunny and warm, such as a windowsill, or in a heated propagator in a greenhouse.

Lovage soon germinates, growing quickly. Once the plant has three to five adult leaves and roots are appearing out of the holes at the bottom of the pots, it can be planted in its final space. Remember, lovage is a big plant! It grows over 2m tall and almost 1m wide and it needs full sun, which can make it tricky to place. Choose your spot wisely.

The plant will die back in winter before re-emerging in spring. When fully established, usually from year two, lovage will send up tall flower stems with yellow umbels that are loved by insects. Eventually these will produce seeds for you to grow more plants if you want to, although one plant is usually enough per household. Lovage is truly perennial and will return every year.

Left Use the fresh parts of the leaves to flavour dishes, such as soups and broths. You can even use them in a variety of salads.

Opposite Lovage forms a substantial upright fountain-shaped plant with plenty of leaves, so you really only need one or two.

Grow as a large vigorous member of an edible perennial plant community. Lovage is so big it will guard its spot and offer other plants support and shelter. This allows you to grow plants next to it which are susceptible to flopping, or other plants that prefer a bit of shade in summer.

Gather

Pick leaves from spring to autumn before top growth dies back as the plant goes into winter dormancy. The best parts are the leaves and thinner bits of stem.

Eat

Use more tender new leaves for salads and sandwiches where you want some greenery with a bit of flavour. Chop and use as an aromatic garnish on chillies, stir-fries and other dishes as you would parsley. Or use as a seasoning alongside Welsh onion (see page 68) or chives (see page 104) to enhance ingredients like tofu and scrambled egg.

Experimenting with unusual plants

If you are unfamiliar with lovage, or any other plants covered in this book, it is worth try experimenting with varying amounts in meals to see how they affect flavour. It's the best way of understanding how plants shape the flavour of different dishes.

Lovage's main use is to flavour and enrich soup, broth, ramen, stews, pies – anything where you'd like to add a deep umami flavour alongside the nutrition of fresh greens. Add a more substantial amount, a good bunch, chopped up. Stems can be added too as they'll be softened after cooking. Incidentally, younger leaf stems can be cooked and eaten in the same way as asparagus but with lovage's flavour.

MINT

EFFORT 4/5
TASTINESS 5/5

Mentha species

Mint is a well-loved herb with a multitude of uses. I love a sweet and refreshing mint tea, which can aid digestion and calm an upset stomach. There are various mint species which all grow in the same way and conditions but have a different flavour.

NUTRITION:
Fibre (high)
Protein (high)
Calcium (high)
Iron (high)
Vitamin A – as beta-carotene (high)
Vitamin B9/folate and other B-vitamins (high)
Vitamin C (high if fresh)
Polyphenols, including flavonoids (high)
Menthol (high)

FAMILY: Lamiaceae
MAX SIZE: 60cm tall, 100cm-plus wide
GROW: year round
HARVEST: spring, summer, autumn
POT-FRIENDLY: yes
SOIL: moisture-retentive
SITUATION: full to partial shade
HARDINESS: H5 (-15°C to -10°C)
ORIGIN: Europe across to Asia, depending on species

Peppermint (*Mentha × piperita*) has soft, pale leaves with a sweeter taste and is often used for desserts, teas and other drinks. Apple mint (*Mentha suaveolens*) tastes similar and is good for the same uses, as is its attractive cultivar 'Variegata', known as pineapple mint. Spearmint (*Mentha spicata*) has darker leaves and a less sweet menthol flavour, so is better used for oils, soaps, and so on.

Grow

Mint grows well in soil that doesn't completely dry out in summer, in full to partial shade. It can grow well in full sun but if the ground does dry out, the leaves can succumb to powdery mildew and even die back from a lack of water, so it is important to water regularly during drought.

Otherwise mint is indestructible. In fact, mint is well known for being too vigorous, so is best restricted in a pot half sunk into the ground to contain those spreading rhizomatous roots. That said, we grow big patches of peppermint and spearmint and though they are a couple of metres wide, they are easily contained by a mown path or other more vigorous plants, like rhubarb and gooseberries.

Left I grow peppermint for tea next to a corner of our polytunnel where I keep it contained by mowing the grass around it.

Mint is so easy to grow from even the smallest scrap, it pains me to ever pay for it. Ask a friend for a division with roots in spring or autumn to plant instead. It will soon grow into a luxurious clump for eating that can outlive us.

Gather

As with most leafy edibles, mint's youngest, freshest leaves are the tastiest and the most tender. By picking the tips of the plant new shoots will emerge lower down for future crops. Being deciduous, mint will die back in winter to return in spring.

Above Spearmint is edible but doesn't taste as nice as peppermint, instead it is used for homemade soap and toothpaste.

Eat

Mint can be eaten raw as a salad leaf, and used as garnish and ingredient. You can even grab a handful of leaves to steep in boiling water to make a fresh mint tea. Chopped mint adds a good flavour to buttery boiled new potatoes. Alternatively, dry lots of leaves through summer to store in an airtight container to make tea in winter. Mint leaves can be frozen for a couple of months too.

Nutrient-dense, if eaten regularly in small amounts mint will contribute to a healthy diet. It contains vitamin A, vitamin B9 (folate) and other B-vitamins, vitamin C, iron, calcium and fibre, as well as menthol and flavonoids that support digestion. Not many nutrients are carried in mint tea, however, which is true for most teas.

OREGANO (WILD MARJORAM)

Origanum vulgare

EFFORT 1/5
TASTINESS 3/5

Known in cooking as oregano, wild marjoram is an edible perennial that's very useful in gardens. It's closely related to culinary marjoram (*Origanum majorana*). The differences are that oregano/wild marjoram is hardy and strong in flavour, whereas culinary marjoram is mild, sweet and tender. Oregano is easier to grow because of its hardiness.

NUTRITION:
Fibre (moderate)
Calcium (high)
Iron (high)
Vitamin A – as beta-carotene (moderate)
B-vitamins (moderate)
Vitamin C when fresh (high)
Vitamin K – K1 phylloquinone (high)
Polyphenols (high)

FAMILY: Lamiaceae
MAX SIZE: 30cm tall, 80cm wide
GROW: spring, summer
HARVEST: year round
POT-FRIENDLY: yes
SOIL: any free-draining
SITUATION: full sun
HARDINESS: H6 (-20°C to -15°C)
ORIGIN: Atlantic Ocean islands, Mediterranean and western Europe across to east Asia

Above A newly planted division of oregano from another part of our garden – aren't free plants brilliant?!

Opposite Like most herbs, oregano has beautiful flowers in a range of colours loved by insects.

As a species, wild marjoram has a fascinating native distribution, from Europe across to Asia, plus some fairly remote islands in the very far north of the Atlantic all the way down to the Canary Islands and Madeira, as well as islands north of Russia. Despite being native to such incredibly distant islands, it never made it as far as Iceland, Greenland or the Americas. The most likely original vector of distribution to these islands would have been seeds dispersed by migratory birds.

Grow

This is a plant-and-forget crop that creates a low, dense mat blanketing the ground. Ground covers like this are invaluable in plant communities for maintaining stability by preventing weed growth. I plant oregano in sunny patches between larger plants where it spreads and weaves into gaps alongside thyme (see page 122).

Either buy a plant or ask a friend for a division. Give oregano some space in full sun and it will soon grow strongly in the first year to about 30–50cm wide, slowly expanding to a 1m patch. Oregano can be grown from seed, but division is easier and faster. Oregano will grow happily in wide pots with a diameter of 20–30cm or more.

The mat of evergreen leaves makes an attractive addition to gardens and a useful spacer between larger plants. In summer, pretty flowers in white to pale pink appear which are adored by pollinators.

The cultivar 'Aureum' has brighter, yellower leaves which, importantly, are milder in flavour and are good for salads and garnish. I grow both this and the species for stronger flavour.

Gather

Pick individual leaves as needed or fresh tips of stems.

Eat

If used dried and ground, oregano is added during cooking. Used fresh, the leaves are usually added towards the end, as a garnish or a tasty salad addition. Oregano is often used as part of a seasoning mix on roast vegetables and meat, and in Italian sauces and pizza.

Oregano is a nutrient-dense herb full of fibre, calcium, iron and antioxidants from polyphenols such as quercetin. Fresh oregano has more vitamin C, but overall the dried leaves are more concentrated in most nutrients. We only eat small amounts of oregano for flavour – as a regular part of our diets it can have valuable health benefits. Dried leaves can be stored in an airtight jar.

Above Over time oregano forms a dense spreading carpet about 10cm tall and evergreen, a very useful trait for reducing unwanted self seeders in dense plant communities.

ROSEMARY

EFFORT 1/5
TASTINESS 4/5

Salvia rosmarinus

I plant rosemary in almost every garden because it is such a beautiful and easy evergreen shrub to grow. Vertical stems of uniform silver-green leaves lend a softness to gardens and are joyful all year round. In spring they are covered in pale blue, pink or white edible flowers that are loved by early bumblebees.

NUTRITION:
Mono- and polyunsaturated fats (low)
Fibre (high)
Calcium (high)
Iron (high)
Magnesium (high)
Potassium (high)
Manganese (high)
Vitamin A – as carotene (high)
Vitamin B1/thiamine (high)
Vitamin C (high)
Vitamin B6/pyridoxine (high)
Vitamin B9/folate (high)
Polyphenols (high)
Phytosterols (high)

FAMILY: Lamiaceae
MAX SIZE: 2m tall, 2m wide
GROW: spring, summer
HARVEST: year round
POT-FRIENDLY: yes
SOIL: any free-draining
SITUATION: full sun
HARDINESS: H4 (-10°C to -5°C)
ORIGIN: Mediterranean

Grow

Although the plant may look tiny in a supermarket pot, rosemary wants to grow into a big shrub, eventually reaching over head height and the same width. So, give rosemary plenty of space to grow, at least 1m or more. Harvesting and clipping can help maintain size while increasing density.

There are many cultivars and forms of rosemary with ever so slightly different growth habits and flavour, though they all taste the same to me. The most notable difference is flower colour and my favourites include blue 'Miss Jessop's Upright' and 'Barbecue', the white-flowered forms Albiflora Group (very chic!) and pink-flowered 'Rosea'.

Rosemary needs free-draining soil in full sun. With these conditions it can tolerate a lot of rain and winter wet down to at least -10°C. We live in a very exposed hilltop location with heavy annual rainfall directly beneath a bog, and all herbs, including rosemary, grow well for us. Rosemary is also very drought tolerant. Such wide tolerance makes it a good contender for climate-change resistance.

Grow semi-ripe cuttings from this year's growth that has started to turn a bit woody. Do this in mid-summer when days are long and warm, cutting 10–15cm lengths. Remove the lower two-thirds of leaves carefully with a knife, or pinch them off with your nails, being careful not to damage the fragile stem. Gently stick the lower

half of the stems into compost, three to five stems per 9cm pot, and water lightly. Place in a bright spot out of direct sunlight and keep the compost only slightly damp. The cuttings should root and start growing again in a month or so. It can help to cover with a transparent lid to lock in humidity until the cuttings root, though rosemary often doesn't need this.

Gather

Snip off shoots as needed. Can be used fresh or dried on a baking tray on a warm, dry windowsill or using a dehydrator. Dried leaves can be crushed and stored in an airtight container. Replace the dried rosemary every six months to maintain the best flavour, though it lasts much longer.

Opposite Rosemary adds an utterly divine aromatic flavour like no other to roast vegetables, potatoes, chips, bread and more.

Above Easy to grow rosemary tolerates most conditions in full sun. As you pick the tips more shoots will grow from the stem below.

Eat

As with many herbs, rosemary is a nutrient-rich herb, but we only eat small amounts at a time compared to other ingredients. Dried leaves are more nutritionally dense per 100g because the water is removed. Using rosemary regularly in meals is beneficial to our diets.

Sprigs of fresh rosemary are often laid on roast vegetables, fish and other meats while cooking to infuse flavour and then removed – good for flavour, but not for consuming its nutrients. The alternative method of pulling off leaves first to add to meals, so they can be eaten with the food, means we digest the leaves.

Potatoes, chips and other roast vegetables covered generously in fresh rosemary leaves and cooked are delicious. Adding rosemary to rice while boiling infuses the flavour and the leaves soften to become more edible. Add to bread mixes, such as focaccia, plus stuffings and sauces. Rosemary even makes a refreshing cocktail ingredient.

SAGE

EFFORT
TASTINESS

Salvia officinalis

With soft, pale green leaves, sage is a beautiful foliage plant for stylish gardens and a perennial edible that's very easy to grow. As with most herbs and spices, sage is nutrient-dense in comparison to other edible crops, but we only eat small amounts at a time. It's therefore important to appreciate that while a single leaf of sage may have a higher proportion of fats, calcium, iron and manganese compared to other plants, the amount we eat at a time is much less. This makes our intake of these components lower than it sounds. The key takeaway is that sage is useful as a regular addition to our diets for both its flavour and nutrients.

NUTRITION: Carbohydrate (high, mostly fibre) Monounsaturated fat (moderate) Polyunsaturated fat (moderate) Fibre (very high) Protein (moderate) Calcium (high) Iron (high) Vitamin K (high) Manganese (very high) Zinc (moderate–high) Copper (moderate–high) Carotenoids (high) Phytosterols (high)	**FAMILY:** Lamiaceae **MAX SIZE:** 80cm tall, 80cm wide **GROW:** spring, summer **HARVEST:** year round **POT-FRIENDLY:** yes, large pots 45cm-plus **SOIL:** any free-draining **SITUATION:** full sun **HARDINESS:** H5 (-15°C to -10°C) **ORIGIN:** western Europe

Above Plant sage in full sun where it can grow to a good-sized bush with plentiful nutritious edible leaves for cooking.

Opposite 'Tricolor' is a mix of green, purple, cream and even neon pink while others available are shades of green, purple or yellow.

Grow

Sage is one of those add-and-forget plants, needing virtually no care from us. Plant in full sun and free-draining soil in the ground or in compost in a large pot. Remember sage wants to become a medium-sized shrub, 60–80cm in height and width – don't be misled by the tiny pots of young plants we buy in supermarkets.

Evergreen in mild areas or sheltered spots, sage may drop its leaves during winter in exposed or colder areas and even experience some stem dieback. New leaves and shoots appear again in spring as weather warms.

I love the straight species, of which there are different cultivars with longer or larger leaf shapes, such as 'Berggarten'. There is also purple-leaved 'Pupurascens', yellow-leaved 'Icterina', and 'Tricolor' with a variegated mix of cream, green, purple and neon-pink. Sages tend to have pale blue flowers in early to mid-summer, though the cultivar 'Albiflora' has pure white flowers. All sage cultivars are edible, and reported to have varying flavour, oil and nutrition. To me they all taste and smell the same.

Grow cuttings of sage easily from spring to mid-summer by taking 10–15cm lengths of semi-mature new shoots with slightly firm woody stems. Cut directly beneath a leaf node and remove the lower two-thirds of leaves with a sharp knife. Poke three to five cuttings into a 9cm pot of free-draining compost and cover with a transparent lid or clear plastic bag. Place on a warm, bright windowsill until roots appear out of the holes at the bottom of the pot(s) in four to six weeks. At this point, plant into individual 2-litre pots to grow larger.

Gather

Pick fresh-looking leaves at any time of year. You can place the leaves in an airtight container or sealable bag and freeze them, or dry them to store in jars. Dry on a tray or use a dehydrator. Store dried leaves whole or ground into a powder, though this is best done when used because whole leaves retain flavour and nutrients better.

Eat

Add sage leaves to flavour butter, breads, including focaccia, and a huge range of dishes, from potatoes, sweet potatoes and rostis to many pasta dishes, as well as tofu, fish and other meats.

SWEET CICELY

EFFORT
TASTINESS

Myrrhis odorata

Originating from many mainland countries in western Europe, sweet cicely is thought to have been spread further north and east by the Romans for its culinary use. With leaves the flavour of sweet aniseed, this wild plant is incredibly easy to grow, useful in meals as a natural sweetener, and looks beautiful in shaded areas of the garden where it can thrive. Cooked as an ingredient in rhubarb compote, its sweet flavour can reduce the amount of sugar needed.

NUTRITION:
Fibre (high)
Calcium (moderate)
Iron (high)
Magnesium (moderate)
Zinc (high)
Vitamin A (moderate)
Vitamin B9/folate (moderate)
Vitamin C (moderate)
Vitamin E (moderate)
Polyphenols (moderate)

FAMILY: Apiaceae
MAX SIZE: 60cm high, 60cm wide
GROW: autumn
HARVEST: spring, summer
POT-FRIENDLY: yes
SOIL: any
SITUATION: full sun to full shade
HARDINESS: H5 (-15°C to -10°C)
ORIGIN: western Europe

Grow

Soft, slightly furry, fern-like leaves unfurl in early spring, followed later in the season by dull white, umbel flowers that are loved by bees, hoverflies and butterflies. Sweet cicely is a beautiful plant which is particularly useful in garden plant communities as an ornamental in shaded spots or beneath larger, more vigorous plants.

Sweet cicely can be bought in pots but is very easy to grow from seed. The large seed-pods can be bought or gathered for free from an existing plant in summer. If the seeds are ready, they will be shiny and black and they should come away from the plant easily without tugging.

To germinate, the seeds need to experience the cold of winter (stratification), which is something you can imitate by placing them in the fridge for a month or two. I find the easiest method is to sow the seeds in a seed tray of compost in autumn, then clearly label and leave it outside somewhere until spring. When the weather warms, the seeds will germinate readily.

Once the seedlings have six to eight leaves, plant in an area of partial to full shade that doesn't dry out completely. Alternatively, scatter seeds in autumn where you'd like them to grow.

Left Sweet cicely's soft leaves have a mild and sweet aniseed flavour that makes a lovely addition to salad or cooked into desserts.

Opposite A wildflower of part-shade or rough verges, sweet cicely is very tolerant of different conditions, with umbel flowers for insects.

Sweet cicely is a very tough plant and doesn't need any particular care. In fact, the only effort needed, aside from harvesting, is to consider cutting off the seed heads to prevent it spreading too much.

Gather

Every part is edible, from the leaves to the stems. The seed-pods are a particularly sweet and tasty treat when picked young and green, before they turn hard. Pick leaves with your hands or cut off as needed. Leaves can be chopped and stored in airtight containers in the freezer for use in cooked meals.

Eat

Chop leaves finely to mix with fruit, or add to savoury salads for a sweet flavour as well as to stewed fruit before cooking. I particularly like sweet cicely as a leafy green in salad – alongside less flavourful salad leaves it balances into a tasty mix. To make a sweet herbal tea, add raw leaves to boiling water and leave to infuse for a few minutes. Seeds can be eaten raw if still soft, which is a gardener's special treat when pottering around outside.

THYME

EFFORT 2/5
TASTINESS 3/5

Thymus species

There are many different cultivars of thyme and these differ in flavour for various uses. I recommend growing a few, so you can taste them first hand, rather than relying on descriptions because our taste-buds and preferences are all different.

NUTRITION:
Fibre (high)
Protein (high)
Calcium (high)
Potassium (high)
Iron (high)
Vitamin B9/folate (high)
Vitamin C (high)
Vitamin K (high)
Polyphenols (high)
Phytosterols (high)
Carotenoids (moderate)

FAMILY: Lamiaceae
MAX SIZE: 20cm tall, 30–60cm wide
GROW: spring, summer
HARVEST: year round
POT-FRIENDLY: yes
SOIL: any free-draining
SITUATION: full sun
HARDINESS: H4 (-10°C to -5°C)
ORIGIN: Europe

Thyme species used in cooking are low-growing twiggy perennials originating from around Spain, France and Italy, such as common thyme (*Thymus vulgaris*) and lemon thyme (*Thymus × citriodorus*) with its lemony aroma and taste. Wild creeping thyme (*Thymus serpyllum*) is also edible, even if its smaller stems are a bit fiddly to pick. This originates from across Europe to Siberia and is a very low-growing, mat-forming species that spreads outwards with white or pink flowers.

Grow

Personally, I like *Thymus vulgaris* 'English Winter' because it has a good, all-round flavour, plus it's larger than creeping thyme but also has a slightly creeping growth, spreading into a mat with dense foliage and beautiful, pollinator-supporting flowers. Useful as another edible ground cover to reduce weeds in full sun and free-draining soil.

Drought tolerant, thyme makes an excellent small evergreen plant to grow in pots or window boxes. Most thyme needs replacing once

Left Did you know that thyme is very easy to grow from seed? Here my whole seed packet has germinated in multipurpose compost.

Opposite Thyme is one of my favourite looking small plants, forming a tight mat of its small leaves with gorgeous summer flowers smothered in pollinators.

it grows straggly after a few years.

Thankfully, thyme can be grown easily from seed in spring. Sprinkle the tiny seeds on top of already damp seed trays of compost. Cover with a transparent lid and they'll soon germinate on a sunny windowsill. Once the seedlings have four to six leaves, gently transplant into their own 7cm pots to grow bigger, eventually planting in their final outdoor spot in late spring. Alternatively, in summer, grow from 10cm-long cuttings, removing the leaves from the lower half and sticking five to seven stems in a 9cm pot of compost. They should form roots after a few weeks.

Gather

Pick sprigs of thyme fresh as needed. They can be dried and stored easily too.

Eat

Add entire sprigs to meals like roast vegetables and remove the woody stems before serving. Or pick off the leaves to sprinkle and leave on the food to consume far more of the nutrients thyme contains. Dried thyme's nutrients are generally more concentrated than fresh. As with most herbs, you can also freeze fresh thyme, and it can last for months like this.

WILD GARLIC

EFFORT 1/5
TASTINESS 5/5

Allium ursinum

Wild garlic leaves are one of my favourite flavours: sweet and mild, and reminiscent of the culinary garlic bulbs from which it gets its name. Being a tough and resilient plant, wild garlic grows in all manner of conditions, making it a useful and much-loved spring foraging crop.

NUTRITION:
Fibre (moderate)
Potassium (moderate)
Calcium (high)
Magnesium (high)
Selenium (moderate)
Vitamin C (high)
Polyphenols (high)
Sulphur compounds – allicin precursors (high)

FAMILY: Amaryllidaceae
MAX SIZE: 20cm tall, unlimited spread
HARVEST: spring
POT-FRIENDLY: yes
SOIL: any
SITUATION: full sun to full shade
HARDINESS: H7 (< -20°C)
ORIGIN: Europe

Grow

One of the easiest plants to grow, the biggest challenge when cultivating wild garlic is actually containing it. The plant produces small bulbs from which new shoots will re-emerge, and it spreads a lot by seed too, which drop around the plant to create an impenetrable carpet.

In gardens this means that wild garlic will create dense ground cover, preventing all other small crops from growing through it, which can be problematic in mixed plant communities.

In our garden wild garlic has colonised the ground beneath our deciduous hedge and it's here that I contain it. The hedge can grow above wild garlic without any problem, and the garlic can make the most of the sunlight before the hedge comes into leaf.

Wild garlic grows leaves in late winter before flowering in early spring. As the weather warms and deciduous trees and shrubs grow their leaves, shading the ground beneath them, wild garlic then goes dormant until next year. This short spring window of growth can be useful for growing in the same ground as plants that emerge later and grow through summer, such as lime tree (see page 60) and Korean aster (see page 52).

To control wild garlic the best method is to dig out excess plants, or try growing larger plants in the same spot that will outcompete it.

Left Wild garlic is useful as a flavour-packed herb while mild enough to use as a salad or stir-fry leaf too.

Right Wild garlic often grows in woodlands.

Below All of the plant is edible and the flowers make a pretty and delicious garnish on salad and soup.

Gather

Pick leaves as needed, always trying to keep a good amount of leaves on the plants to help them build up energy. Leaves can be stored in the fridge for a few days but are best eaten fresh. The edible flowers can also be picked.

If you're worried that wild garlic may take over your garden (and with good reason because it probably will), remember that it grows all over Europe in the wild in large quantities. Forage it from big wild colonies instead.

Eat

Add wild garlic to sandwiches, salads and stir-fries for a mild, sweet and fresh garlic flavour. Flowers can be added to salads and soups as a decorative and tasty garnish.

Leaves also make a delicious garlicky pesto. Take a large handful of wild garlic leaves, a heaped tablespoon of roasted pine nuts or walnuts, and a heaped tablespoon of grated Parmesan cheese, then blitz in a food processor. Cover with olive oil and a squeeze of lemon juice, stir and then either use fresh or store in the fridge. Both the leaves and flowers have strong antioxidant properties.

OTHER PERENNIAL HERBS WORTH A TRY

- Lemon balm *Melissa officinalis*
- Lemon verbena *Aloysia citrodora*
- Nepal pepper *Zanthoxylum alatum*
- Russian tarragon *Artemisia dracunculus*
- Scented pelargonium *Pelargonium* spp.
- Society garlic *Tulbaghia violacea*

Nuts

All our protein requirements can be obtained from plants, with one of the key sources being the humble nut. Nuts are large seeds, which means they are packed full of nutrition, including lots of protein, beneficial fats and, in some cases, good carbs. Lentils, beans and pulses also contain protein, but these are currently annuals, making nuts a prized perennial crop for forage gardens. Perennial nut trees are top of the list to broaden food crops for humanity around the world and, thankfully, they are incredibly easy to grow and harvest. Some nuts are suitable for small gardens, while others are huge with yields to match, better suited to parks, farms, schools, and business and community gardens.

Left We grow lots of hazel trees around our small farm, coppicing them to keep them manageable and to use their stems to grow beans up. Many of them grow and crop beneath larger trees as part of the understorey.

ALMOND

EFFORT 3/5
TASTINESS 5/5

Prunus amygdalus and *Prunus × persicoides*

Packed full of protein, good fats, fibre and lots of vitamins and minerals, including magnesium, which is thought to help us sleep, almonds are one of my favourite nuts. I can, and literally do, snack on them every day.

NUTRITION:
Monounsaturated fats (high)
Fibre (high)
Protein (high)
Magnesium (high)
Phosphorus (high)
Potassium (high)
Calcium (moderate)
Iron (moderate)
Zinc (moderate)
Manganese (high)
Copper (moderate)
B-vitamins, including vitamin B9/folate (moderate)
Vitamin E (high)
Phytosterols (moderate)

FAMILY: Rosaceae
MAX SIZE: 5m tall, 4m wide
HARVEST: autumn
POT-FRIENDLY: no
SOIL: any
SITUATION: full sun
HARDINESS: H5 (-15°C to -10°C)
ORIGIN: cultigen from Transcaucasus

Botanically almonds are a drupe, not a nut, which means that, like a mango, they grow on the tree as a fruit with a seed inside a hard shell in the middle. Except in almond's case, we eat the seed, rather than the flesh.

Grow

Given almonds take many years to reach cropping size, they are best grown from cultivated plants rather than from seed to ensure you know exactly what you're planting. *Prunus × persicoides* 'Ingrid' is a reliable heavy cropper for warmer and drier areas, while *Prunus × persicoides* 'Robijn' is considered better for colder and wetter areas. You only need one almond tree because they are self-fertile, allowing insects to pollinate flowers on the same tree.

Almond trees are hardier than many realise and can grow in more northerly parts of the northern temperate world. The reason we think of them as warm-country trees is because they need warmth to crop reliably, so they're planted more in warm countries. Being one of the earlier trees to blossom, spring frosts can kill the flowers before they've had a chance to be pollinated, which means no nuts.

Give your almond tree a helping hand by planting it somewhere sheltered and with full sunlight all day to help power the tree and warm the soil. As our climate warms, almonds may become more useful

Above Almond blossom has the most incredible sweet scent in warm spring sunshine.

Opposite Trees need a long hot summer to produce a good harvest of almonds.

towards the poles and harder to grow in drier regions nearer the equator.

Even in a normal climate, almonds are one of those crops I feel are worth growing if you have space because they may crop in warm years. While it may not be every year, it's something to look forward to: how wonderful to have a surprise crop of your own almonds. They are also very beautiful blossom trees with a wonderful almond scent.

Gather

Wait until the green fruits split open in autumn, a sign they are ripe and tasty. Collect the fruits and dry in the warm inside for a few weeks, such as a sunny windowsill. Once the fruit is completely dry, the nut (or drupe) should come away more easily.

Store dried almonds in an airtight container somewhere cold and dark.

Eat

Almonds make a delicious snack raw whenever you are feeling peckish. Roast them slightly in the oven until golden and to intensify the flavour, adding a satisfying crunch. Roasted almonds make a good chopped addition to salads. Grate, chop and grind raw almonds to add to various dishes, from cakes to biscuits.

HAZELNUT: COBNUT AND FILBERT

EFFORT ●●●○○
TASTINESS ●●●●●

Corylus avellana and *Corylus maxima*

Hazels are one of the smaller nut trees and can be pruned annually to around head height to fit small gardens and to make harvesting easier. Size, flavour, nutrition and ease make them a super perennial edible for future gardens.

NUTRITION:
Monounsaturated fats (high)
Fibre (high)
Protein (high)
Copper (high)
Manganese (high)
Magnesium (high)
Phosphorus (high)
Vitamin B6/pyridoxine (high)
Vitamin B7/biotin (high)
Vitamin B9/folate (moderate)
Vitamin E (high)

FAMILY: Betulaceae
MAX SIZE: 8m tall, 8m wide (prune to maintain at 2m tall, 2m)
HARVEST: autumn
POT-FRIENDLY: no
SOIL: any
SITUATION: full sun
HARDINESS: H6 (-20°C to -15°C)
ORIGIN: Europe (*Corylus avellana*), north-west Balkan Peninsula (*Corylus maxima*)

I've always loved hazelnuts – raw or roasted, they're tasty and crunchy. Thankfully, hazelnuts love us back; they're particularly rich in vitamins B6 and E, biotin (vitamin B7), manganese, copper and monounsaturated fats. These each contribute toward a healthy body by helping our heart and immune system and also healthy ageing by reducing oxidative stress.

Grow

Corylus avellana (often called cobnut) is a wild deciduous tree species from across Europe, while *Corylus maxima* (called filberts) is a very closely related species originating specifically from the north-west Balkan Peninsula. The main differences are that *Corylus maxima* has larger leaves, larger nuts and the green husk grows longer around and beyond the nut. On *Corylus avellana*, the husk is shorter, so the nut protrudes. Many cultivars available today are hybrids between these two species, and sometimes hybrids with other species from around the world.

While hazel is easily grown from seed – I grow wild *Corylus avellana* in hedgerows – for food production, I concentrate on cultivars bred for much greater yield. 'Cosford Cob' is very sweet and very heavy cropping, while 'White Avellana' is particularly useful for yields in colder regions. Although all advice is that hazels prefer neutral or alkaline, free-draining

Grow your own plant supports

Coppiced hazel stems make an excellent sustainable source of 2m+ poles to form structures for climbing plants such as beans, sweet pea and squash. Cut every five to seven years for strong, tall poles. Their twiggier parts cut to 50–100cm in height, called pea sticks, make excellent supports for annual climbing peas and around smaller perennials in windy spots.

soil, they grow well on our mildly acidic heavy soil which does get very wet in winter.

Hazels tolerate partial shade and growing beneath larger trees, where they will still crop. They do crop much better in full sun, however. Self-fertile, hazel can be grown singly – and you're likely to have a wild hazel nearby anyway – but because they are wind-pollinated, it can increase pollination and therefore yield to grow two or more together.

Hazels grow up to 6m or so eventually. You can restrict them to about 2m by pruning the ends of the main stems in winter while the tree is dormant. Alternatively, coppice every seven years or so, which obviously stops the crops until stems grow back, or pollard to about 1.5m from ground level to restrict height while speeding up regrowth to cropping size.

Gather

Collect nuts in autumn when they start to come away easily from the husk and begin to drop. Another clue is when squirrels start eating them: be quick or they'll gobble the lot! Kept somewhere dry and cool, hazelnuts can be stored for 12 months. Alternatively, crack open the shell and freeze the edible kernel.

Eat

Hazelnuts are edible raw or can be toasted for 5–10 minutes at 180°C (fan oven) until golden brown. Personally, while I enjoy raw hazelnuts, I love their flavour and crunch when toasted. I eat hazelnuts as a snack alongside other nuts. Use in salads and chopped into dishes, cakes and biscuits. Raw hazelnuts can also be soaked overnight, blended and then strained to make milk. Press using a screw press while raw or lightly roasted to produce oil.

Right Hazelnuts are ready to pick when they turn brown and come away from the husk easily.

Opposite Hazelnuts collected from our wild trees and those in our edible hedges.

MONKEY PUZZLE

EFFORT ●○○○○
TASTINESS ●●●●●

Araucaria araucana

Around the time I was born, in the early 1980s, British gardeners had gone crazy planting a spiky oddball in front gardens: the monkey puzzle tree. A conifer that resembles a cactus and totally out of place in the British countryside, most of those who planted it didn't realise their pot of joy would grow into an absolute whopper!

NUTRITION: Despite limited credible data, it is known to be rich in carbohydrates (mainly starch) and fibre.

FAMILY: Araucariaceae
MAX SIZE: 30m tall, 10m wide
HARVEST: autumn
POT-FRIENDLY: no
SOIL: any
SITUATION: full sun
HARDINESS: H7 (< -20°C)
ORIGIN: Chile and Argentina

Forty years later and many of those trees now tower over the houses to which they were planted far too close. But those avant-gardeners gifted us one of the greatest perennial edibles for future generations. As the Indigenous people of Chile and Argentina have always known, monkey puzzles produce abundant delicious and nutritious nuts.

Grow

Monkey puzzles are wind-pollinated and dioecious, which means a plant is either male or female and both are needed for pollination. Unfortunately, there is currently no way of knowing whether monkey puzzles are male or female until they flower, which can take 20–40 years, by which point they're a huge tree... It's pot luck if your tree will produce nuts.

Best advice if you fancy growing one is to go for it, then wax lyrical about its edible produce to your neighbours. If you can encourage someone else to plant one, you may hit on the perfect duo. The more monkey puzzles in an area, the more wind-blown pollen and chance of nuts. If you have access to a large park or community garden, consider planting a grove of three or more. Although tall, when mature they are very narrow and drop all their lower branches, forming an umbrella shape, which allows light in for smaller trees and shrubs beneath.

Right Monkey puzzle nuts look and taste like a cross between pine nuts and chestnuts.

Monkey puzzle trees can be grown from fresh seed, 3cm deep in a 9cm pot of compost kept somewhere warm. In milder climates they self-seed and grow naturally.

Gather

Female monkey puzzles produce large, spherical cones, containing 200-plus edible seeds, and have a lifespan of well over a thousand years. This is an amazingly sustainable food source – when the ripe cones drop to the ground, they contain the nuts ready to collect. Use gloves to handle the spiky cone and pull out the slightly winged seed cases. Leave these to dry on a windowsill, then cook (see below) and peel off the brown case to reveal the light seed inside. The edible kernels look like giant pine nuts.

Eat

Monkey puzzle nuts are edible raw or cooked. They're firmer and more flavourful when roasted for 5 minutes or until golden brown at 180°C (fan oven). They can also be boiled for 10 minutes. Keep the winged shell on while cooking as it's easier to peel off once cooked. Taste and texture is a cross between a roast chestnut and a large pine nut. Eat as a snack, whole or chopped in salads or other meals where other nuts are used. Dehydrated, the nuts can be ground into piñon flour.

Above Mature trees grow many cones with the long male cones producing pollen carried in the wind.

Below Round female cones produce seeds enclosed in a winged case that peels away easily when roasted.

PINE NUTS

EFFORT 4/5
TASTINESS 5/5

Pinus pinea

Buttery and sweet, pine nuts make a delicious addition to pesto, pasta dishes and salads. They are energy-dense and nutrient-rich, and filled with good fats, protein and various minerals.

NUTRITION:
Monounsaturated fats (high)
Protein (moderate)
Magnesium (high)
Phosphorus (high)
Potassium (moderate)
Iron (moderate)
Copper (high)
Zinc (high)
Manganese (extremely high)
Vitamin B1/thiamine (moderate)
Vitamin E (high)

FAMILY: Pinaceae
MAX SIZE: 25m tall, 20m wide
HARVEST: autumn
POT-FRIENDLY: no
SOIL: any
SITUATION: full sun
HARDINESS: H4 (-10°C to -5°C)
ORIGIN: southern Europe to Lebanon

Grow

All pine nuts are edible but due to their fiddliness when gathering and shelling, species with larger nuts are used. The stone pine (*Pinus pinea*) is the main species grown in Europe and we focus on this here.

Other parts of the world grow species suited to their climate, such as *Pinus sibirica* in Siberia, *P. koraiensis* in Asia, *P. armandii* in Central China, and *P. monophylla* and *P. edulis* in the US. There are many others and it's worth researching the best species with the biggest nuts for your area.

Pinus pinea is an evergreen tree for full sun, which grows up to 25m tall and has a wide spreading canopy that gives its nickname of umbrella pine. It is drought tolerant, making it useful for warming regions of the temperate world.

Grow from seed, either bought or collected, and plant 2cm deep into a 10cm pot of compost. This can be done in spring, though it can help germination to sow in autumn and leave outside over winter. This gives the seed a blast of cold that can help germination in spring, a process called stratification. It's fun growing pine trees from seed: the seedlings look like cute mini-trees.

Left Pine nuts are seeds from cones encased in a light shell that's fiddly to remove but worth it.

Stone pine will need to be 10–15 years old before it starts cropping but will live for hundreds of years.

Gather

The first step for gathering pine nuts is easy: look for freshly fallen cones in summer and autumn, then bash them onto a sheet to knock the nuts out (the sheet allows you to pick them up easily).

Step two is the tedious bit; the light edible seed is inside a brown shell that needs removing. There's no escaping this. The process is fiddly and you can either snip off the wide end of the shell to pick the nut out, or gently roll them with a rolling pin to crack the shells, though this can break the nut inside.

You can store pine nuts raw in an airtight container in the fridge for a couple of months, or freeze for up to six months.

Eat

Eat as a snack or add to meals raw or lightly toasted, either in an oven or pan-fried for a few minutes, to enhance flavour, being careful they don't burn.

Below Mature trees can produce hundreds of cones filled with the edible seeds each year.

SWEET CHESTNUT

EFFORT 2/5
TASTINESS 5/5

Castanea sativa

We all know sweet chestnuts 'roasting on an open fire' from the song, but it's time we got better acquainted with this once popular crop. Sweet chestnuts are packed with carbohydrates, which are important for energy, and were once considered a core food.

NUTRITION:
Carbohydrate (high)
Fibre (high)
Potassium (high)
Phosphorus (high)
Copper (high)
Manganese (high)
Vitamin B1/thiamine (high)
Vitamin B6 (high)

FAMILY: Fagaceae
MAX SIZE: 35m tall, 30m wide
HARVEST: autumn
POT-FRIENDLY: no
SOIL: neutral, acidic
SITUATION: full sun
HARDINESS: H6 (-20°C to -15°C)
ORIGIN: Balkan Peninsula to northern Iran

Sweet chestnuts are beautiful large trees – their deep-fissured bark twists around the trunk as though spiralling out of the ground, and the glossy, oblong-lanceolate foliage with toothed edges is among my favourites of deciduous leaves, turning yellow before falling in autumn.

Male and female flowers appear in summer on striking long catkins on the same tree, pollinated by wind and insects. The female parts become the nut. As a hardwood that can happily be coppiced, sweet chestnut has also traditionally been used for fence posts and firewood.

Grow

Sweet chestnut trees are very hardy and drought tolerant, making them an important crop for drier regions, including those becoming drier due to climate change. They can live for thousands of years, making them a truly sustainable and easy food source and stable wildlife habitat. Space is the main consideration when growing, as sweet chestnuts are huge, eventually reaching upward of 20–30m tall – not one for small gardens but worth planting in parks and other large community spaces.

You can grow sweet chestnut from fresh seed planted about 3cm deep, but it is better to choose cultivars bred for specific qualities. I grow 'Marron de Lyon' for a more compact tree, reliable cropping and single kernels (the nut). 'Marigoule' is a self-fertile hybrid between *Castanea*

Left Edible sweet chestnuts have single oblong leaves and spikier cases than superficially similar but poisonous conkers.

five years. Size can be restricted to approximately 4m tall and wide with pruning, pollarding or coppicing every seven to eight years, but be aware that this will impact cropping in the immediate years afterwards.

Gather

When the spiky sweet chestnut seed cases begin to split in autumn, revealing the shiny, brown nuts inside, they're ready to harvest. Wear thick gloves to handle the spikes, prizing cases open to collect the nut. You may need a ladder to reach those still on the tree. Sweet chestnuts can be stored in the fridge for a few weeks or in the freezer for six months. If freezing, first cut a slit into the nut, so they are ready to roast from frozen.

sativa and the Japanese chestnut (*Castanea crenata*), which is useful if you can only grow one. Choosing cultivars like these with single large kernels per case is better for food because they are easier to peel, whereas the true species usually produces multiple small, fiddly nuts.

Plant somewhere with enough space in full sun and protect the young saplings from rabbits and deer. Water in the first summers until established. Once the tree is a few metres tall and the trunk is 10cm-plus in diameter, protection can be removed. Bought cultivars can start cropping after three to

Above Sweet chestnut are beautiful trees, their long glossy leaves are particularly ornamental.

Right Wild trees produce multiple small chestnuts per case whereas cultivars tend to contain a single larger seed.

Eat

Sweet chestnuts can be eaten raw by cutting the hard brown case open to reach the nut inside. They taste much nicer after roasting. First, carefully cut a long slit along one side of each chestnut's brown case, place on a baking tray and roast at 180°C (fan oven) for 30 minutes or until darkened, but not burned. Remove, then allow to cool sufficiently for the split case to be opened to remove the delicious nut. For advanced chefs, sweet chestnuts can be ground to make a flour for baking by first boiling and then dehydrating before milling.

Note that although horse chestnuts (known as conkers) look very similar, they are actually not closely related and the horse chestnut (*Aesculus hippocastanum*) is not edible.

WALNUT

EFFORT 2/5
TASTINESS 5/5

Juglans regia

Walnuts are high in energy and contain lots of healthy fats, especially polyunsaturated fats such as Omega-3, which are understood to lower cholesterol, reducing the risk of heart disease and stroke. Although walnuts are another large tree – as are most hardy nuts except hazels – eventually growing to over 20m in height and width, it is well worth trying to find space for them in local community gardens and parks for future generations to forage.

NUTRITION:
Polyunsaturated fats (high)
Monounsaturated fats (moderate)
Fibre (moderate)
Protein (moderate)
Magnesium (high)
Copper (high)
Phosphorus (high)
Zinc (moderate)
Manganese (high)
B-vitamins, including B9/folate and B7/biotin (moderate)
Vitamin E (moderate)

FAMILY: Juglandaceae
MAX SIZE: 30m tall, 20m wide
HARVEST: autumn
POT-FRIENDLY: no
SOIL: any
SITUATION: full sun
HARDINESS: H6 (-20°C to -15°C)
ORIGIN: Turkey to Lebanon and Western Himalayas

Grow

It's possible to grow walnuts from fresh seed by sowing into a 20cm pot of compost, 8cm deep (with 3cm of compost above the nut). Leave the seed outdoors protected from wildlife and it should germinate in spring. Walnuts self-seed and have been found growing in the wild around Europe in hedgerows and woodlands.

However, it is far better to plant cultivars selected for quality and high-yielding crops. 'Broadview', 'Buccaneer', 'Rita' and 'Lara' all come recommended. While walnuts are self-fertile, cropping is much improved with partner trees. Try growing a mix of different cultivars to see how each fairs and add to the world's knowledge by growing walnuts in your region.

Ultimately, walnuts crop best where it is sunniest and warm, so plant in a bright spot to power the growth of those big nuts. It's said that walnuts are best in southern regions, but our friend Jenny Slaughter of Grow + Graze has had her young walnut produce nuts in Yorkshire at over 300m.

Prune the top off the central leading stem at waist- or chest-height. This will help restrict the overall height of the tree by encouraging branching.

Below Walnuts grow in smooth green cases that split open when the seed is ripe.

Gather

Collect walnuts as they fall from the tree, as this is when they are ripe. The race is on to beat the squirrels! Walnuts fall with a thick, green husk around the familiar woody shell. This should peel away easily but can stain your hands green, so wear gloves. Remove all the green, fleshy husk completely before storing.

Walnuts kept in their woody shells can be stored in an airtight container somewhere cool and dark for two to three months. Alternatively, remove the shells and store in an airtight container in the fridge for 6–12 months. Or store shelled walnuts in a container or bag in the freezer for 12 months or more.

Eat

Removed from their shells, walnuts can be eaten raw or cooked. I like roasting them for 5 minutes or so in the oven or air fryer at 180°C until golden brown, as this brings out a delicious flavour and improved texture. Walnuts are delicious chopped and added to salads or stir-fries for a bit of nutrient-packed crunch.

Below Our neighbour Jenny Slaughter grows this fruiting tree in her food forest at over 1,000ft next to a windswept moor.

Flowers

It's easy to admire the beauty of flowers and overlook their worth as a nutritious food crop. Many perennial flowers grown in gardens are edible, ranging from quite tasty to delicious. They can be sweet or peppery. Some are comparable to substantial salad leaves; others are small and best used as a garnish. All contribute to our nutritional intake, while adding exciting colours and flavours to meals and drinks. With the right selections, harvesting flowers to eat is the same as deadheading, which will encourage more to grow.

Above *Monarda didyma* 'Panorama' has edible petals that bring colour and sweet flavour to salads while the leaves taste of bergamot.

DAHLIAS

EFFORT 2/5
TASTINESS 3/5

Dahlia species

I love growing dahlias for their bold and structural flowers in every colour of the rainbow. Their petals and tubers are edible and while they won't set your dinners alight with flavour, they are easy to grow. It would be worth the world's food growers revisiting dahlias as a perennial edible.

NUTRITION:
Petals (varies by cultivar):
Vitamin C (high)
Polyphenols (high)

Tubers (varies by cultivar):
Carbohydrate – mainly inulin (high)
Fibre (moderate)
Protein (moderate)
Potassium (high)
Magnesium (high)
Calcium (high)
Phosphorus (high)
Zinc (high)

FAMILY: Asteraceae
MAX SIZE: varies by cultivar
HARVEST: summer, autumn
POT-FRIENDLY: yes
SOIL: any
SITUATION: full sun
HARDINESS: H4 (-10°C to -5°C)
ORIGIN: Mexico and occasionally further south for some species

What's more, if you grow single-flowered cultivars with one set of petals, bees and butterflies will love having access to lots of nectar and pollen late in the season. Dahlia petals are actually sterile ray florets around a central yellow collection of tiny fertile florets. On the showy double flowers, fertile florets are bred into rays, reducing the amount of pollen and nectar available to insects.

Grow

Plant new tubers or cuttings in 2-litre pots inside in spring to protect them from frost until they are about 30cm tall. In early summer, when frosts are over, plant the dahlias in their final space. I find dahlias are hardy even in our exposed garden, returning most years. If you live in colder areas, provide extra protection by covering with straw or a mound of compost, or dig tubers up to store inside over winter. Always try some outdoors over winter to test hardiness in your garden.

Dahlias come in a bewildering array of cultivars with different heights, colours and shapes. To make life easier, I recommend cultivars less than 70cm tall that don't need support and are single-flowered for wildlife, such

Left Dahlias come in a huge range of exciting colours, sizes and flavours – the petals and tubers are the tastiest parts.

as my favourites 'Waltzing Mathilda' and 'Bishop of Canterbury'. Have fun choosing.

Cuttings are easy. In spring, when new shoots appear, gently scrape back the soil and use a sharp knife to cut some shoots off, taking a bit of the tuber with them – essentially cutting off the bit of tuber the shoot is attached to. This can be planted 1–2cm deep into a 2-litre pot of compost, covered with a transparent lid or bag, and kept on a warm, bright windowsill. In a few weeks new leaves will grow, signalling that roots are growing too. Transfer the young plants to individual pots until they're big enough to go outside. Small- to medium-sized dahlias are easy to grow in 30–40cm pots of compost.

Gather

Cut off flowers and pluck the petals to eat. Cutting off the flowers will encourage replacements all summer. In autumn you can dig up the whole plant to access the tubers to eat. Replant one or two tubers, making sure they have growing points, and they should return next year.

Eat

Petals are eaten raw as a salad item, making for very colourful salads! They taste a bit like a cross between a pea and lettuce to me and contain vitamin C and varying levels of the polyphenols flavonoids and anthocyanins. Tubers are useful as a starchy alternative to potatoes, only with a blander flavour. Peel, boil or roast them. Both petals and tubers taste subtly different between cultivars.

Right 'Waltzing Mathilda' has warm peach-coloured single flowers produced all summer accessible to pollinators.

Below It's easy to propagate lots of free dahlias by taking shoot cuttings in spring.

DANDELION

EFFORT
TASTINESS

Taraxacum officinale

There are thousands of species of dandelion around the world and many are edible, but I'm going to focus on the easily identified common species *Taraxacum officinale*. Considered a weed by many, dandelions are beautiful flowers in spring and early summer, providing much-needed sustenance for early insects. They contain a lot of sustenance for us too, an unlimited, ever-growing crop of food.

NUTRITION:
Leaves:
Fibre (high)
Calcium (high)
Iron (high)
Potassium (high)
Vitamin A (high)
Vitamin C (high)
Vitamin K (high)
Phytosterols (high)
Polyphenols (high)

FAMILY: Asteraceae
MAX SIZE: 50cm tall, 25cm wide
HARVEST: year round
POT-FRIENDLY: yes
SOIL: any
SITUATION: full sun
HARDINESS: H5 (-15°C to -10°C)
ORIGIN: Europe across to Asia, depending on species

Grow

Dandelions grow everywhere there's sunshine. So prolifically that many people want to see the back of them and are constantly digging them out. I've learned to love them – in fact, I've always loved them – their big, fluffy, golden flowers are so happy, and the spherical seed clocks are still granting my wishes to this day.

In our garden I rarely remove dandelions because, actually, they are the least problematic wildflower. Their rosettes of leaves may spring up everywhere, but they are flat and small, and soon covered by larger emerging perennials. In the meantime, they serve the purpose of covering soil to stop other plants jumping into that space. A natural ground cover that the bees love.

For eating, I wouldn't have a specific dandelion patch, but instead just grow in wild grass areas, lawns, various corners of the garden, and even centre stage on verges for a golden blast. I'll forage around to find them.

Gather

Being evergreen, dandelion leaves can be picked all year, though in winter they become a little battered by wind and tough with age. In spring, tender new leaves emerge and these are the best: young leaves are sweeter, turning a little bitter when older (story

Left All parts of a dandelion are edible including the roots. I tend to use the leaves and flowers most in salads.

Left En masse dandelions create a spectacular display when they emerge in early spring.

Below The flowers can be eaten raw or fried in batter for a sweet vegetable starter or side dish.

of my life). Pick leaves as needed. Flowers are also edible, so you can pick those too. If you are digging dandelions up, save the biggest roots to clean and use. A hori-hori levers the roots out easily.

Eat

Dandelion leaves are like wild lettuce if you're sticking to the sweet younger leaves. These can be used in sandwiches, mixed in a salad or fried for a minute like spinach. Flowers can be fried or battered, or pick off the petals to sprinkle into salad raw; they're sweet.

Roots can be roasted like a thin parsnip and they can also be used to make an alternative caffeine-free coffee. For this, clean and leave the roots to dry for a few days first. Then chop into 1cm pieces and roast on a low heat, around 160°C (fan oven) for 30 minutes until chocolatey brown and dry. When cool, the chopped root can be ground. To make a cup of substitute coffee, add a heaped tablespoon of the ground roots to a cup of boiling water, infuse for a few minutes and then strain.

DAYLILY

EFFORT
TASTINESS

Hemerocallis species

Daylilies obtained their name because each flower only lasts for a day, which is useful for ornamental edible gardens because you can enjoy the flowers through the day, then eat them with dinner! The more you pick, the more will grow.

NUTRITION:
Flowers:
Potassium (high)
Calcium (high)
Iron (high)
Vitamin A (high)
B-vitamins (moderate)
Vitamin C (moderate)
Polyphenols, including flavonoids (moderate)
Carotenoids (high)

FAMILY: Asphodelaceae
MAX SIZE: 80cm tall, 80cm wide
HARVEST: summer flowers, year-round leaves
POT-FRIENDLY: yes
SOIL: any
SITUATION: full sun to partial shade
HARDINESS: H7 (< -20°C)
ORIGIN: Alps, Siberia to temperate east Asia (depending on species)

It can be unnerving eating flowers and petals if you're mainly used to eating leaves, but remember that broccoli and cauliflower are flower-buds too. I'm glad I tried daylily flowers, as their large, succulent petals are sweet and delicious with just enough lettucy crunch. They are, however, even easier to grow than these crops.

Grow

Daylilies are available to gardeners in a wide range of flower sizes and colours, from yellow and orange to red, pink and white. Most of these *Hemerocallis* species, hybrids and cultivars have edible flowers, tubers and leaves. They include orange *Hemerocallis fulva*, yellow *H. citrina* and yellow *H. lilioasphodelus*, but check carefully first. Lilies, in a different genus (*Lilium*), are likely not edible.

Our garden in Yorkshire came with a well-established clump of orange *Hemerocallis fulva* 'Flore Pleno', a double-flowered cultivar with many or all of its stamens replaced with additional petals, increasing petal yield. It grows in fairly heavy shade and flowers from mid- to late summer. Even when the ground dries in heatwaves, 'Flore Pleno' continues to flower and look vibrant. I've since tried it in full sun where it grows just as well, demonstrating that this is a tough, resilient food crop for future climate chaos.

Part of the resilience of daylilies is due to their root tubers, which are underground energy storage

Above Create a talking point with colourful and sweet petals of daylily and other edible flowers in your salads.

Opposite Double flowers of 'Flore Pleno' means extra petals with just enough pollen for insects, and the buds are delicious too.

organs. These starchy, thickened roots gradually spread outwards from the parent plant, producing new shoots.

You can take divisions from the plant in spring or autumn to grow more. This is an easier and faster approach for reaching harvesting age than growing from seed. Divisions are genetic clones, whereas seedlings can vary in look and flavour (useful for breeding if you'd like).

Daylilies grow in different soil types, moisture conditions and light levels. So, they make a flexible addition to plant communities in various conditions. Try growing some plants in different spots in your garden to test their resilience. Generally, they will grow better with some soil fertility and if they don't completely dry out in summer.

Note: The pollen of daylilies can be very poisonous for cats, so do not grow where cats roam.

Gather

Pick young leaves by hand and don't pick the older ones as these are stringy. Tubers can be dug up and washed like small potatoes, again using the young tubers as the older ones are tough. Daylily flowers are the main event for me. Pick each open flower by hand – they snap away easily – or select the unopened flower-buds. Picking the flowers for eating will encourage the plant to produce more flower stems, thus prolonging the harvest.

Eat

Petals and buds can be eaten raw as a delicious salad addition, or fried with or without tempura batter. Young leaves are cooked and eaten like spinach or kale. The nutty-flavoured tubers are cooked and eaten in the same way as potatoes.

ELDERFLOWER

EFFORT 🍃🍃🍃🍃🍃
TASTINESS 🍃🍃🍃🍃🍃

Sambucus nigra

Elderflower is my ultimate cordial. Sweet and subtle, perfect with a bit of fizzy water, it's the divine taste of summer. As if it couldn't be any better, you can make litres of the stuff yourself with so little effort – even I can be bothered to do it. Another reason for growing elderflower is to cultivate jelly ear fungi (see page 166).

NUTRITION:
Very little nutrition is obtained from elderflowers, but they contain vitamins A and C, trace levels of B-vitamins and minerals, plus polyphenols.

FAMILY: Viburnaceae
MAX SIZE: 8m tall, 6m wide (easily pruned)
HARVEST: early summer
POT-FRIENDLY: no
SOIL: any
SITUATION: full sun to partial shade
HARDINESS: H6 (-20°C to -15°C)
ORIGIN: Europe

Grow

I would not be without elderflower's contemporary style in early summer, with its mix of green to creamy white discs creating a spectacular lacework. Then in autumn come the black-purple berries loved by birds.

Easy to grow, plant an elderflower and it will flourish without any problem. Elderflowers never grow that tall, but if space is an issue, they are very tolerant of pruning. Keep to head height by sawing off all branches to a central waist-high stump every few years in winter while the plant is dormant. It may not flower that summer but will in subsequent years.

Hardwood cuttings can be grown from 20–25cm lengths of stem in winter, with buds at the top and bottom of the stem. Bury the bottom half of the stems in soil, or three to five cuttings in a 2-litre pot of compost outside, and they should root in spring.

Gather

Pick 20 to 30 of the biggest flowers on a dry day the moment the buds open and look fresh, placing them gently in a basket or bag. You'll see powdery pollen, which is where most of the elderflower flavour is held. Place the flowers to one side for half an hour or so to give any insects a chance to leave, and don't wash the flowers; otherwise you'll wash away the pollen and flavour. Trim off most of the big bit of stalk, but don't worry about the smaller bits near the flowers.

Left Elderflower cordial is quick and easy to make, letting you bottle the beautiful taste of summer.

Above The best elderflowers to eat or use for cordial are those that have just opened and are a vibrant, creamy colour.

Below Elderflowers can also be dipped in a light batter and fried, making wonderfully crisp, fragrant fritters.

Eat

To make elderflower cordial, heat 2 litres of water in a saucepan with 2kg of caster sugar, stirring until the sugar has dissolved, and then allow to cool. Add 25–30 flower-heads, the zest of two lemons, and 100g of citric acid as an optional preservative. Cut the rest of the rind off the lemons, slice and put this in too. Cover and leave to infuse for 24 hours, then strain through a clean cloth to separate the liquid. Funnel into bottles and store for up to six months in a cool pantry or fridge. The mixture can also be frozen. Alternatively, fry elderflowers whole in tempura batter and serve as a snack, starter or side dish.

Elderflowers are thought to contain some vitamin C and flavonoids, but the amount in cordial will be limited, with more in fritters. Homemade cordial is likely to retain a little more nutrition than shop-bought versions.

VIOLA SPECIES

EFFORT
TASTINESS

Viola cornuta, *Viola odorata* and *Viola riviniana*

Violas are essential edible flowers – they are simply so easy to grow and have a wonderfully sweet flavour for use in salads and garnishes. I've highlighted three perennial species here: sweet violet (*Viola odorata*) and dog violet (*Viola riviniana*), which originate from all across Europe down to North Africa, and horned pansy (*Viola cornuta*), originating from France and Spain.

NUTRITION: Too little credible data available

FAMILY: Violaceae
MAX SIZE: 20cm high, 50cm wide (or more)
HARVEST: summer, autumn

POT-FRIENDLY: yes
SOIL: any
SITUATION: full sun to partial shade
HARDINESS: H7 (< -20°C)
ORIGIN: Europe to North Africa, depending on species

Above *Viola tricolor* is a wild annual species that self sows each year, so it acts like a perennial (see page 22).

Below *Viola cornuta* 'Minor Alba' needs full sun where it will create a mound of flowers in summer.

All three species form dense spreading mats, covering the ground and helping fill out plant communities. They tolerate some shade, making them useful space fillers that can withstand growing between and around bigger edible perennials. Despite highlighting these three for their reliability, all *Viola* have edible flowers and you can try one of the many garden hybrids too.

Grow

Violas are a doddle to grow. Plant them where you like and they'll begin to spread outward slowly over the years, filling in gaps. When they've spread a fair way, you can dig out a clump with a trowel to move elsewhere for more.

Try growing violas in 20–30cm pots or window boxes for edible colour all summer. They just need a bit of sunlight and moisture, so as not to dry out.

Viola odorata, the sweet violet, has a slight scent on warm days and is fairly shade-tolerant, making it a good choice for shadier gardens. Cultivars of all

Viola exist in different shades of white, blue, purple and pink.

Gather

Pick the flowers as needed. It is better to use them straight away, though they will keep in a sealed bag or airtight container in the fridge for a day or two.

Eat

Use the flowers to bring a little colour and excitement to salads or as a garnish on other meals. They also make lovely decorations on cocktails and other drinks, as well as desserts.

Below *Viola odorata* flowers in spring with a sweet scent and forms reliable, dense, evergreen ground cover in shade.

WILDFLOWERS

EFFORT ●●○○○
TASTINESS ●●●●○

Various species

I want to highlight three of my favourite wild plants with edible flowers and leaves which I feel are easy and tasty enough to add to your grow wishlist. Many other wildflowers have edible parts, but always check with an expert first if you want to try eating them – see also common bistort (page 40) and sorrel (page 62).

NUTRITION:
Not enough credible data, but all three of the wildflowers described here contain a range of different nutrients and polyphenols in varying amounts, meaning they can make a useful, if modest, contribution to diets.

FAMILY: Various
MAX SIZE: 60cm high, 60cm wide (or less)

HARVEST: spring, summer, autumn
POT-FRIENDLY: yes
SOIL: any
SITUATION: full sun (partial shade for primroses)
HARDINESS: H7 (< -20°C)
ORIGIN: Europe and temperate regions of Asia (*Leucanthemum vulgare*), Europe to western Turkey (*Malva moschata*), Europe, western Asia and parts of North Africa (*Primula vulgaris*)

Grow

Ox-eye daisy (*Leucanthemum vulgare*) is a large daisy in the Asteraceae family which is super easy to grow in sunny spots. Once planted, it will naturally self-seed gently around the place but never seems to take over completely. It forms dense rosettes of leaves that guard their spot in a plant community, before sending up flower stems from spring until late autumn – now that's flower-power! Leaves, flower-buds and flowers are all edible.

I find musk mallow (*Malva moschata*) to be the tastiest mallow in the Malvaceae family and one of the prettiest too. Grow in full sun where, like the ox-eye daisy, it will gently spread outwards into a clump. It does self-seed but not as much as ox-eye daisies. The leaves are a tasty salad leaf and the petals are edible too.

Primrose (*Primula vulgaris*) in the Primulaceae family has tasty edible flowers in spring, which are slightly sweet. Its leaves are also edible, but I find they can be quite bitter – as always, the golden rule with wild foraging is that younger leaves are less bitter. Primroses are very tolerant of shade in summer because they evolved growing around deciduous woodland edges. They too will self-seed once established, though they're very easy to divide as well.

All three plants are excellent in plant communities due to their tough tolerance of competition.

Below Musk mallow is one of my favourite edible wildflowers with good salad flavour to its leaves and petals.

Above Ox-eye daisy leaves and flowers are edible – both have a slight floral taste.

Below Primrose flowers and leaves can be added to salad or as a garnish, the flowers being sweeter than the leaves.

Gather

Pick leaves and petals as needed. Removing the entire flower will encourage the plant to produce more. The whole flower-head is edible on all three plants.

Eat

I use these wildflowers in salads for a boost of colour and different nutrients. Ox-eye daisy flower-buds can be pickled to use like capers. Musk mallow leaves are small and heavily divided, but I feel are one of the best perennial salad leaves.

OTHER PERENNIAL EDIBLE FLOWERS WORTH A TRY

- Bergamot *Monarda* spp.
- Clover *Trifolium pratense*
- Common daisy *Bellis perennis*
- Creeping bellflower *Campanula rapunculoides*
- Gorse *Ulex europaeus*
- Hibiscus *Hibiscus syriacus*
- Honeysuckle *Lonicera periclymenum*
- Hyssop *Agastache foeniculum*
- Roses *Rosa* spp.

Fungi

Fungi are amazing organisms and sit in their own unique kingdom alongside plants and animals (they are biologically closer to animals than plants). There is a vast and fascinating world of fungi to explore, with species in all shapes, colours and sizes. The mushrooms we see are usually the reproductive parts that release spores into the air and germinate under very unique conditions. Most of a fungus consists of fine filaments called hyphae which together form the thicker mycelium unseen in the ground or within plant tissue and dead wood. Sometimes fungi feed on dead material, while others form beneficial partnerships with living plants. Like plants, some fungi are edible and tasty, as well as full of protein and other nutrients. I've included a handful of the more common and easily identifiable fungi for beginners to forage. A number of these can be grown in gardens.

Safety tips: Like plants, many fungi are poisonous and because they can be hard to identify, it is important that you only eat them when you're absolutely sure what they are. **Always:**

- Seek reliable identification (ask an expert if in any doubt).
- Avoid inhaling spores.
- Check both the inside and outside of fungi for insects before bringing them home.
- Leave enough mushrooms behind, so the fungus can reproduce.

Opposite Jelly ear, *Auricularia auricula-judae*, grows on dead wood of living elder. You can encourage this habitat through annual pollarding.

BEEFSTEAK FUNGUS

EFFORT
TASTINESS

Fistulina hepatica

Seeing your first beefsteak fungus is one of those 'is this real?' moments. Starting red-orange and more rounded when young, as it matures it spreads out, growing slightly thinner and flatter into a bracket that turns deep red to resemble a giant tongue. The top can feel slightly wet or slimy and looks very similar to a piece of meat, hence the name. Give one a squeeze and it will ooze droplets of red liquid that look exactly like blood. Isn't nature bizarre!

NUTRITION:
Carbohydrate (moderate)
Protein (low)
Iron (moderate)
Potassium (moderate)
Vitamin C (high)
Phenolic acids (moderate)

FAMILY: Fistulinaceae
MAX SIZE: 6cm thick, 25cm wide

GROW: late summer, early autumn
HARVEST: late summer, early autumn
POT-FRIENDLY: not applicable
SOIL: not applicable
SITUATION: full shade
HARDINESS: mycelium H6 (-20°C to -15°C), fruiting body H4 (-10°C to -5°C)
ORIGIN: temperate regions

The beefsteak fungus is parasitic (drawing nutrients from a host) and grows on living and dead oak wood or occasionally sweet chestnut, usually near the bottom of the trunk. Its underside is a pale white-cream with sponge-like pores from which the spores are released. While there are many bracket fungi, it's hard to mistake them for beefsteak, from its host trees to appearance – others don't ooze a blood-like liquid!

Grow

Look around woodlands or parks for beefsteak fungi on oak and sweet chestnut trees in late summer to early autumn. Only pick them if you find a good number in an area; otherwise leave them to spore and reproduce.

If you live in an area where beefsteak fungi grow, and you have space, you could try growing an oak tree. These can be coppiced or pollarded every seven years or so to restrict their size. Or you could ask a tree surgeon for some spare oak logs to place in a dark, damp corner somewhere, then wait and see if beefsteaks arrive.

Left One of the telltale signs of identification is that when squeezed it will ooze a blood-like red liquid.

To speed the process along, it is possible to buy plugs inoculated with beefsteak fungus spores. You drill holes into logs of oak, the size of the plugs you want to push inside, then leave the logs outside and wait. If they take, beefsteak fungi will grow out of the logs.

Gather

Beefsteak fungi can be eaten young and old, but the sweet spot is somewhere in between. This gives you more mushroom without them being too tough. A good-quality beefsteak mushroom is when it's reasonably large, about 20–25cm across, but still looks fresh and in good condition. Snap these off the tree or log it's growing on. Remember only to take one and leave any others in the ecosystem, allowing them to reproduce with spores.

Above Beefsteak is a bracket fungus with a unique look of steak from the top and when sliced, though it doesn't taste like beef.

Eat

You can eat beefsteak mushroom raw or cooked. It doesn't taste like beefsteak; instead it has a slightly sour taste from its acidic content and dense mushroom texture. Don't be put off! Slice thinly and add raw to a salad with other ingredients and sauces. Or cook the mushroom by slicing thinly again and sautéeing or grilling (covered in olive oil) until golden brown, perfect added to creamy pasta dishes.

To reduce sourness, slice and soak the mushroom in cow or plant-based milk for a few hours, then drain and cook. It can be a good mushroom to cook in stews and casseroles.

CHICKEN OF THE WOODS

EFFORT
TASTINESS

Laetiporus sulphureus

What came first, the chicken or the mushroom? Probably the mushroom, as chickens evolved relatively recently by comparison. Chicken of the woods resembles a giant, flattened chicken nugget. Unlike beefsteak fungi (see page 156), chicken of the woods *does* live up to its name, with an uncanny taste and texture reminiscent of chicken. It's remarkable.

NUTRITION:
Carbohydrate (high)
Fibre (moderate)
Protein (moderate)
Potassium (moderate)
Phosphorus (moderate)
Iron (high)
Zinc (high)
Copper (high)
Vitamin D (if exposed to sun)

FAMILY: Laetiporaceae
MAX SIZE: 6cm thick, 25cm wide

GROW: summer, autumn
HARVEST: summer, autumn
POT-FRIENDLY: not applicable
SOIL: not applicable
SITUATION: full shade
HARDINESS: mycelium H6 (-20°C to -15°C), fruiting body H3 (-5°C to 1°C)
ORIGIN: northern temperate regions

Chicken of the woods is an easy bracket mushroom to spot because it has a distinct look. It is large and a vibrant orange-yellow, and has wobbly, rounded edges, usually with multiple brackets which protrude from deciduous hardwood trunks, including those of oak, beech, chestnut and others. Timing wise, you'll spot this mushroom in late summer into autumn; it is perennial and usually crops every year. All of these qualities make it a good beginner fungus to identify, and it also happens to be tasty and filling.

Grow

Abundant in deciduous wooded areas, this is one fungus for your foraging lists where you'll have a good chance of spotting a patch in the wild. Once you know where it grows, you can revisit each year in summer and autumn during warm wet spells.

You can also buy plugs inoculated with chicken of the woods spores to grow in your garden, making sure they are raised from fungi originally relatively near to your area, so as not to introduce random strains into the wild. When growing fungi in your garden from introduced spores, I would always make sure the supplier sourced the spores from a local strain and suggest picking all fruiting bodies to eat to reduce spread; unlike in the wild where it's important to leave many to reproduce.

Ask a tree surgeon for a large log of oak or other hardwood that is at least 20cm in diameter and 100–150cm long; chicken of the woods is a big fungus and needs a lot of wood to produce a good crop. Drill holes into the log for the plugs and hammer them in, then leave outside in a shaded damp corner, either on the ground or partially buried to secure vertically. Eventually the fungus should appear.

I'm interested in recreating the habitat chicken of the woods needs in gardens and community gardens to see if it will eventually appear naturally one day (alongside others in this book). For this, you should grow deciduous hardwoods like oak, beech, alder, chestnut or other hardwood trees. These are all easily coppiced (cut to the ground) or pollarded (cut higher up) when young and the trunk is at least 10–15cm in diameter. This restricts the tree's size and produces a supply of deadwood. Chicken of the woods could naturally appear if it's already growing nearby.

Gather

Gather chicken of the woods when it's on the younger, plump side and tender. As they get older, the brackets flatten and grow tougher, so are no fun to eat. However, they are delicious when plump and tender – simply snap off a bracket and take it home. Always remember to leave more brackets than you take for the fungi to reproduce from spores. Cut the brackets into strips and put in a sealed bag or airtight container to store in the freezer for up to a year.

Eat

Chicken of the woods must be well cooked before eating and can be used to replace chicken or tofu in any dish. Snap into nugget-sized pieces and discard tougher bits towards the short stem. Pan-fry for at least 10 minutes, adding a little water initially, which will evaporate. Then fry on both sides until golden brown. Alternatively, first cover in breadcrumbs or a little cornflour for a crispy coating. They can be used for all sorts of dishes.

Right You'll find chicken of the woods growing fairly high on dead or partially dead deciduous hardwood trees, such as oak.

Opposite Chicken of the woods is a large vibrant yellow or orange with wavy plump edges reminding me of chicken nuggets.

FIELD BLEWIT

EFFORT (1 of 5)
TASTINESS (4 of 5)

Collybia personata

Field blewit is an easy-to-identify mushroom with very smooth, grey-brown caps, cream to grey-white gills, and vertical fibrous stems (usually with blue-lilac streaks). The stems are usually thicker at the base and the inner flesh is off-white when sliced. The cap starts slightly convex and rounded before flattening once mature.

NUTRITION:
Not enough credible nutritional information

FAMILY: Clitocybaceae
MAX SIZE: 6cm tall, 12cm wide
GROW: winter
HARVEST: winter
POT-FRIENDLY: not applicable
SOIL: acidic, water-retentive
SITUATION: full to partial shade
HARDINESS: mycelium H6 (-20°C to -15°C), fruiting body H4 (-10°C to -5°C)
ORIGIN: Europe

Very much a fairytale mushroom, it's easy to imagine fairies and gnomes living near the field blewit. It can be found growing in fairy rings on short grassland. I'll let you work out if it's good or bad luck to enter the ring!

Grow

I often come across field blewits exactly where the name suggests they will grow: in fields such as meadows or pastures. I'm sure this fungus grows in longer grasslands but is obviously more visible when the grass is short over winter, which is the time it grows. Field blewits seem to grow in sunny patches of grass not too far from woodland, though there doesn't seem to be a clear reason for this proximity to woods.

Field blewits are one of the fairy ring fungi that form rings of mushrooms in grassland (not all fairy ring fungi are edible, so be sure of your ID). Fairy rings are formed as the fungus grows outwards, so the actual living part is inside the fairy ring beneath the grass. Fruiting parts form on the outer reaches of the larger body below ground.

Left Field blewit gills are closely packed and start off white before turning a pale pink or buff colour.

Above A key identifying feature of field blewit is the brown cap that looks like a pancake with vivid purple stems underneath.

Left Look out for field blewits growing in short grassland or lawn, often in fairy circles with brown caps.

It is possible to propagate field blewits by transferring a small amount of soil with the fungus to a suitable new area. Obviously, it is irresponsible to do this from the wild where they play an important role in ecosystems, so I strongly advise against that. However, if someone you know has some in their garden, it's worth giving it a go. Dig a trowel-sized piece of soil along the outer edge of the fungus and plug it into a prepared hole of the same size in your lawn or field, if you have one. Alternatively, scattering spare fruiting bodies on grass may work, as you are allowing the spores to wash into the soil when it rains.

Gather

Lift each mushroom from the stem or cut the stem at ground level with a sharp knife. Field blewit is edible when cooked at any stage, but for the most mushroom wait until the cap is beginning to flatten and enlarge.

Eat

Field blewits must be cooked to avoid stomach upsets, though once cooked are totally edible and delicious! All you have to do is slice and cook as you would any mushroom.

GIANT PUFFBALL

EFFORT
TASTINESS

Calvatia gigantea

I like puffball fungi, mainly because of their cute name. Giant puffballs are smooth, rounded mushrooms that can look like eggs or balls on the ground. Spores develop inside until eventually the top splits open and the spores are literally puffed into the air when raindrops hit the outside case or wind lifts them out. If you spot an open one, try tapping it lightly with your finger to see it puff.

NUTRITION:
Fibre (moderate)
Protein (moderate)
Polyunsaturated fatty acids (high)
Phenolic compounds (moderate)

Limited reliable data, but likely nutrient-dense

FAMILY: Agaricaceae
MAX SIZE: 40cm in diameter (occasionally up to 80cm)

GROW: summer, autumn
HARVEST: summer, autumn
POT-FRIENDLY: not applicable
SOIL: any
SITUATION: full sun to full shade
HARDINESS: mycelium H6 (-20°C to -15°C), fruiting body H2 (1°C to 5°C)
ORIGIN: temperate world

Above Giant puffballs can be sliced into large mushroom steaks. It is edible when the flesh is completely white, with no spores or gills.

The giant puffball is the most easily identifiable because of its size, growing from 10cm all the way up to 80cm in diameter, and is often mistaken for a football. Its size and texture make it a prized mushroom among foragers in the summer and autumn when it appears.

Grow

You can find giant puffballs growing on grassland or open areas of woodland. They can't be confused with other mushrooms of their shape and size, making them a good beginner fungi to forage.

The giant puffball, like all edible puffballs, is used while young *before* it starts producing spores inside. At this point, when sliced in half, the entire mushroom should be firm and white inside. All of the mushroom is edible – if you find a whopper, that's a lot of mushroom!

Like many ground-dwelling mushrooms, giant puffballs require specific conditions, which we don't truly yet understand. That said, it is always worth waiting for a giant puffball you find to produce spores, then taking some of those spores to your garden by scooping into a jar or plastic bag. Be careful not to breathe in the spores, as large amounts can cause a respiratory illness called Lycoperdonosis. Although this is treatable, you don't want to have it. Place in a watering can with water and stir. Then pour the mix around a spot with identical conditions to where you found the puffball – that is, open grassland or lawn.

As with most mushrooms, although giant puffballs produce seven trillion spores on average, they have extremely poor success rates, which explains why we aren't overrun with puffballs. This makes it a case of try and try again until hopefully you have your own puffball.

For this reason, although fairly common and producing loads of spores, because of its low reproduction rate, you should always leave at least one giant puffball to reproduce. If there's only one, it's better to leave it than eat it.

Below Although giant puffballs aren't common, they are easily found and identified by their huge size.

Gather

Ripe giant puffballs are pure white all the way through, with no spores or gills – a solid mass of white mushroom. If they have any spores or discolouration, leave and look for other ripe bodies elsewhere. To gather, simply tilt and lift; they'll snap away from tiny filaments attached to the underground mycelium.

Eat

All of the giant puffball is edible, including the skin, though you can peel this off if it is tough. Slice the puffball into steaks of mushroom and fry as it is, or first cover in batter and breadcrumbs. It can also be chopped into smaller pieces and cooked like any other mushroom. Due to its size and firm texture, I definitely enjoy the large steak option as a fairly unique addition to meals.

GOLDEN CHANTERELLE

EFFORT
TASTINESS

Cantharellus cibarius

Chanterelle mushrooms are one of the best wild mushrooms to eat. While there are various species of chanterelle, here I will focus on the common golden chanterelle (*Cantharellus cibarius*). With a slightly apricot scent, these golden yellow mushrooms are distinctly trumpet-shaped with slightly wavy edges to their caps. Gills are simple and tend to run from the edge of the cap into the stem. The flesh is firm and white inside. Although common, chanterelles can still be overharvested, making it important to leave many more mushrooms to spore and reproduce than you take.

NUTRITION:
Fibre (high)
Iron (high)
Phosphorus (moderate)
Potassium (high)
Zinc (moderate)
Copper (high)
Manganese (moderate-high)
Vitamin B2/riboflavin (moderate)
Vitamin B3/niacin (high)
Vitamin B5/pantothenic acid (high)
Vitamin D (very high)

FAMILY: Cantharellaceae
MAX SIZE: 10cm tall, 10cm wide
GROW: summer, autumn
HARVEST: summer, autumn
POT-FRIENDLY: not applicable
SOIL: acidic, water-retentive
SITUATION: full to partial shade
HARDINESS: mycelium H6 (-20°C to -15°C), fruiting body H2 (1°C to 5°C)
ORIGIN: Europe to Mediterranean

Grow

Chanterelle are mycorrhizal fungi, which means their thread-like hyphae attach to the roots of plants – in the case of chanterelles to trees, thought to include oak, beech, birch, spruce and pine. This relationship between the fungus and the tree does not harm either and is beneficial, with both organisms exchanging nutrients. In many cases, mycorrhizal fungi allow the tree to absorb nutrients it may not otherwise be able to and vice versa. It is also through these fungal networks that scientists now believe trees can communicate by exchanging different chemicals.

Due to this complex relationship, introducing and growing chanterelles at home is a long-term and uncertain project. Even if successful, it can take five or more years for the mushrooms to appear. Therefore, chanterelles are best treated as a forage item to look for in woodlands on acidic soil from mid- to late summer into autumn. Protect patches you find by safeguarding the trees and not overharvesting – leave lots of mushrooms to reproduce.

If you would like to have a go at introducing chanterelles to your garden, first you need the trees mentioned above to be well established and you must have naturally acidic soil (which rules out gardens on neutral or alkaline soil). As the trees are all large, this is a project best suited to big gardens and community gardens – and be very patient!

Place spare, locally sourced fruiting bodies of chanterelles on the soil around tree bases, and with the right conditions their spores may take. Keep trying and in future years you could be lucky enough to find some growing. Alternatively, in some areas it's possible to buy young tree saplings already inoculated with chanterelles, and these just need planting.

Opposite Few things are as delicious as a meal made with freshly gathered golden chanterelle.

Above Golden chanterelle are pale orange in colour, grow in damp mossy woods, have a mild scent of apricots and a wavy trumpet shape with gills running down the stem.

Gather

Chanterelles can be found in mossy and damp areas of woodland on acidic soil. The mushrooms lift away easily from the ground. Always remember that these are the reproductive parts of the fungus, making it important to leave a good number to increase the population. You can dry chanterelles in a dehydrator or on a sunny windowsill, but they taste much nicer fresh.

Eat

Trim off any slightly harder bits of the stem (not too much, as the stem is edible) and pan-fry in a little olive oil, whole or chopped, for a few minutes until just turning a golden brown. Add to pasta dishes, eat on toast or combine with vegetables in a stir-fry. Chanterelles are a treat, so I prefer simple dishes to enjoy their flavour.

JELLY EAR FUNGUS

EFFORT
TASTINESS

Auricularia auricula-judae

Also known as wood ear, it helps to think of the jelly ear fungus as seaweed; otherwise it's wobbliness might put you off! This easy-to-identify cup fungus grows all year round, being most prevalent fully hydrated in the colder, wetter months of winter. Few fungi grow in winter that look anything like jelly ear, making it a perfect beginner mushroom.

NUTRITION:
Carbohydrate (high)
Fibre (moderate)
Protein (moderate)
Iron (low)
Sodium (low)
Potassium (high)
Calcium (high)
Phosphorus (moderate)
Vitamin B1/thiamine (moderate)
Vitamin B2/riboflavin (low)
Vitamin B3/niacin (moderate)

FAMILY: Auriculariaceae
MAX SIZE: 0.5cm thick, 7cm wide
GROW: year round
HARVEST: year round, mainly winter
POT-FRIENDLY: not applicable
SOIL: not applicable
SITUATION: sun or shade
HARDINESS: mycelium and fruiting body H6 (-20°C to -15°C)
ORIGIN: Europe

You'll find fruiting mushrooms on the deadwood of elderflower trees (*Sambucus nigra*; see page 148), which helps with identification, and occasionally some other deciduous trees. I usually spot them on the dead branches of a growing tree. Living up to their name, the dark brown, cupped fruiting bodies really do look like ears, always hanging down towards the ground.

Scientifically called *Auricularia auricula-judae*, the genus name *Auricularia* comes from *auricula*, the Latin for 'ears', while the specific epithet *judae* is earned because it was once said that Judas hanged himself on an elderflower tree, which is where the fungus is most likely to be found.

You've likely eaten jelly ear or one of its closely related cousins in Asian stir-fries or soups – they're often the finely sliced dark mushrooms with a satisfyingly rubbery crunch (trust me – it's good!).

Grow

Invite jelly ears into your garden by establishing the habitat they need: dead elderflower wood. While they can grow on other hardwoods, they prefer elder, and in our garden they grow on dead sections of various living elder trees. Growing deadwood may be an oxymoron, but it is possible and important because jelly ear is saproxylic, meaning it feeds only on deadwood.

Above Freshly gathered jelly ears can be fried whole or sliced.

Elderflower trees (see page 148) grow easily in full sun to partial shade. Allow them to grow into full trees and wait – they tend to grow new branches, while some occasionally die back without harming the plant. To speed the process along, deploy the old technique of pollarding, where you cut off branches while dormant in winter to encourage fresh new growth in spring. This inevitably leaves patches of wood to die at the base of the old branch, and this is where the jelly ears will grow. Deadwood on a living tree.

If you've seen jelly ears growing in your area, it will only be a matter of time before they find your tree. Try placing fresh fruiting bodies of jelly ear onto the dead sections of tree to help spores take.

Gather

Identifying jelly ear fungi is easy. They're dark brown, smooth (unless very dry), cup-shaped like an ear, always facing down, and grow on elder trees. In winter, when hydrated and easy to spot, few other mushrooms look like them. Pick the freshest-looking mushrooms, which are slightly lighter in colour. They pull away easily. Wash them.

Eat

Rich in potassium, fibre, calcium and protein, jelly ear is a nutritious crop. Freshly picked jelly ear can be chopped, removing tougher stems, and cooked in the same way as any other mushroom: fried or boiled for 3–5 minutes until tender, or added to stews and stir-fries. Don't eat jelly ear raw. Dehydrate to store indefinitely, then rehydrate as needed by soaking the mushroom in water for an hour or so (you can also gather jelly ear dried and crispy in summer). Although they don't have a strong natural flavour, their cooked texture provides a great contrast in dishes, having a little more bite than a normal mushroom.

Below Jelly ear fungi are easily identified by colour and the downward hang of the fruiting body, and they are almost always found on elderflower trees.

OYSTER MUSHROOM

EFFORT
TASTINESS

Pleurotus ostreatus and *Pleurotus pulmonarius*

Oyster mushrooms can be found growing all around the temperate Northern Hemisphere, mainly on deciduous hardwood trees and dead logs, especially beech. Two common species are *Pleurotus pulmonarius*, known as the pale or summer oyster mushroom, and *Pleurotus ostreatus*, which is commonly called the grey or winter oyster mushroom. The summer and winter names relate to when they are more usually seen.

NUTRITION:
Fibre (high)
Protein (high)
Potassium (high)
Magnesium (moderate)
Phosphorus (moderate)
Iron (moderate)
Manganese (low)
Vitamin B2/riboflavin (moderate)
Vitamin B3/niacin (moderate)
Vitamin B5/pantothenic acid (moderate)

FAMILY: Pleurotaceae
MAX SIZE: 2cm thick, 15cm wide
HARVEST: summer, autumn, winter
POT-FRIENDLY: not applicable
SOIL: not applicable
SITUATION: full shade
HARDINESS: mycelium H6 (-20°C to -15°C), pale oyster fruiting body H2 (1°C to 5°C), grey oyster fruiting body H4 (-10°C to -5°C)
ORIGIN: northern temperate regions

Individually shaped like a shell, oyster mushrooms grow in clumps and have very little stem. Their gills, the thin, papery parts underneath the cap that produce spores, clearly run from the edge of the cap all the way down the stem. Summer oysters are pale cream to white, while winter oysters are brown to blue-grey. There are other oyster species, depending on your area.

Grow

It is possible to buy home kits to grow oyster mushrooms indoors, which are really fun and do work. If you do this, try to buy the ones with species native to your area to avoid unwanted species escaping into the wild. However, indoor kits tend to produce one or two harvests before being thrown away. I'm more interested in creating the right habitats for fungi to grow outside.

I've watched beech trees being pollarded and cut down, the deadwood left on the ground to decompose. Two to three years later and those logs were home to hundreds of oyster mushrooms because the species grow locally to where the trees were cut. If you live near a wild spot with oyster mushrooms, you can replicate this in a garden.

Ask a tree surgeon for some spare beech logs and lay them down in a cool, dark, damp corner of your garden. Alder, oak, birch and willow logs also work. If you are lucky, at some point in the future oyster spores will land and grow on the logs.

Alternatively, to make your own luck, order some dowl plugs inoculated with spores native to your area. Drill holes in the log to the same diameter as the plugs, then insert the plugs and leave to grow.

All of the above deciduous hardwoods are easy to grow and coppice every seven years or so – which means cutting them to the ground to reshoot from the base. This gives you an unlimited supply of hardwood logs to keep growing your own oyster mushrooms.

Gather

Gathering oyster mushrooms is as easy as pulling them away from the log. Only pick those that look young and fresh. Never take all of the mushrooms; leave some to spore for future generations of fungi. Oyster mushrooms can be dried in a dehydrator and stored in an airtight jar in a cool, dark place. Rehydrate in room-temperature water for an hour before use.

Eat

Oyster mushrooms are easily fried for 5–10 minutes until golden. They are delicious as a protein in stir-fries and ramen, or used as a pulled pork alternative in sandwiches.

Right Winter grey oysters are distinctive in shape with a smooth top, curved edge and gills running down the stem.

Opposite Pale oysters are more likely found in warmer summer and autumn months, starting rounded before turning more wavy.

PARASOL

EFFORT
TASTINESS

Macrolepiota procera

Parasols are a large and choice mushroom to forage and eat. They taste typically mushroomy, but are a little more on the sweeter side. All in all, substantial and delicious! Among the more fairy-tale-looking fungi, they are typically mushroom-shaped – every bit the umbrella that the name suggests.

NUTRITION: Despite limited credible data, it is known to contain protein, copper, iron, zinc.

FAMILY: Agaricaceae
MAX SIZE: 40cm tall, 25cm wide
HARVEST: summer, autumn
POT-FRIENDLY: not applicable
SOIL: free-draining
SITUATION: full sun to full shade
HARDINESS: mycelium H6 (-20°C to -15°C), fruiting body H2 (1°C to 5°C)
ORIGIN: temperate world

Grow

Found growing in open grassland or dappled open areas of deciduous woodland, parasols are fairly common. Though not common enough to strip the wild of every one that you see – always leave some to reproduce to keep their numbers high.

Identifying parasols is fairly easy, but beware, as there are many large mushrooms that look very similar to the untrained beginner and are poisonous. Always seek a second opinion from a fungi expert before eating one until you are absolutely sure.

The way to identify parasols is first by their size, shape and location; they are large and grow in open grassland or light areas of woods. They are often in a small clump or form a loose fairy ring as the underground fungus ages. When parasols first emerge, the cap is egg-shaped with brown scales. As the cap grows, it becomes whiter because the flesh between the scales expands. The stem has similar brown scale markings all the way down.

Once in its classic parasol shape, the cap expands horizontally, which causes the ring attachment to the stem to tear away from the cap remaining on the stem. A key characteristic of parasol mushrooms is that this ring is usually detached and easily moved up and down the stem.

Left Parasol mushrooms are identified by their large size, brown scales on top and importantly, a ring on the stem that is detached.

Opposite Find parasol mushrooms in grassland and open woodland areas.

Underneath, the gills are a very pale off-white with a hint of brown-cream. On top the scales are still a recognisable pale brown. The middle of the cap has a raised bump called an 'umbo'. Its flesh when cut is white and stays white.

Trying to grow parasols in your garden is a challenge as with most ground-dwelling fungi because it's hard to know if the conditions are right. However, there is no harm in placing a cap producing spores on an open grassy area and hoping they grow in future.

Gather

Pick by hand or cut the stem at ground level. These will store for a few days in the fridge in a paper bag. The mushrooms can also be frozen raw and cooked later, or dehydrated to rehydrate later for use.

Eat

Parasols are sliced and cooked as with any other mushroom. I like to savour the unique flavours of wild mushrooms and favour an uncomplicated recipe that doesn't overpower them, such as a simple pasta or fried with fresh sourdough toast.

Studies do suggest parasols can absorb high levels of metal minerals, depending on the soil, especially cadmium for which caution may be needed. Don't gather near busy roads, industrial areas, contaminated soil or where soil is known to be heavy in natural metals. The advice is not to overconsume parasols, especially if used dried when their content becomes significantly concentrated. Instead, you should spread out meals using them and collect from unpolluted areas.

Note: Unfortunately, nutritional information on parasol mushrooms is very limited, as with so many other wild-foraged foods. This is because food composition research is expensive and few companies are interested in analysing food we can pick for free! It is therefore best to assume for now that parasols are likely fairly similar in nutritional value to other mushrooms.

OTHER EDIBLE FUNGI WORTH A TRY

- Penny bun/Porcini *Boletus edullis*
- Dryad's saddle *Cerioporus squamosus*
- Hedgehog fungus *Hydnum repandum*
- Scarlet elf cup *Sarcoscypha austriaca*
- Shaggy ink cap *Coprinus comatus*

Prisilla Manove

Social entrepreneur – Goroka, Papua New Guinea

I've followed Prisilla's work in Papua New Guinea for years, where she works with communities who grow some of the world's finest coffee and other perennial crops.

Can you tell me about your work and communities you work with?
My ancestors have been farming for thousands of years. We're in the highlands, here in Goroka, at 1,500m, and it gets cooler in the mountain ranges. I work with smallholders in vegetable farming and commodity farming. Here, 97 per cent of the land is owned by traditional landowners; all the tribes and communities own land. Everyone is involved in subsistence farming, which has been a way of life for thousands of years. The problem is empowering farmers to take produce to the market – I want to create economic opportunities for rural people.

Below 'Robusta' is a bitter coffee bean regularly used in instant coffees, accounting for a whopping 40 per cent of global coffee production.

The old ways are now regarded as more cutting edge and better than we've managed in the West.
Intensive Western farming is the antithesis of what I want in my country. If you look at coffee plantations, for example, the majority were built by commercial interests during colonial times. But land with a coffee plantation was originally owned by families from different clans. When the colonialists arrived, they said, 'We'll take this land.' When they left, Indigenous farmers went back, reclaiming their land and started farming. But there was a problem with farming to the previous standard because people didn't know how to farm coffee. It wasn't a traditional crop like taro or yam, sweet potatoes and sugar cane. We have so many varieties of sugar cane, beans, sweet potatoes, greens. Everything is edible. That's the problem.

Above Taro is a root vegetable, similar to potato, though it needs warm conditions and will not survive frost.

People think, 'Everything grows on my land. Why do I need to commercialise? I'm good.'

Are some clans open to your ideas?
A lot want a better life for themselves, especially with technological advances and the internet. When we talk about getting a better life, they understand that they need to get into farming, like coffee farming. Not so much vegetable farming because we don't have the logistical support or infrastructure to support commercial agriculture at that scale.

Why is coffee more important for selling?
Since there aren't enough incentives to support vegetable farmers, people don't take vegetables to markets as much as they would commodities like coffee. Here in the Eastern Highlands, we have 2.5 million households who live on coffee. But we're not big coffee drinkers. Some of us have to drink more coffee for everyone else... I drink a lot of coffee!

What conditions does coffee thrive in?
Coffee grows in cool regions of tropical climates in the 'coffee belt' around the equator, where cacao is also grown, between the Tropics of Capricorn and Cancer. There are two main varieties: 'Robusta', which grows in the lowlands along the coast where it's hotter, and 'Arabica', which grows in the highlands, probably at 1,000m and above. Coffee requires a lot of rainfall and prefers the shade. Around the plantations, shading trees are planted along the coffee lines to protect the saplings. As the trees grow bigger, they protect the coffee from the sun. Different soils bring out different flavours. Coffee grown on limestone has a more acidic flavour than coffee grown on volcanic soil, which is different altogether. I've met people who are very pedantic about their coffee in Europe or Asia. In the West, people talk about coffee and community in coffee shops, but for us, it's a livelihood. By being part of that process, by supporting our coffee, you're supporting our communities.

By communities do you mean beyond the farmers?
Yes, as the whole process entails the extended family. Our Melanesian society is about familial ties and strengthening customary obligations. Coffee strengthens community and culture.

Are other perennial crops grown that are important to your communities?
Taro, sweet potatoes, yams and bananas. We also have sago, a big palm tree that grows in swampy places in the lowlands. They cut the tree down, pulp the bark, extract the water and make it into a starchy powder. In Asia, they use it in desserts. But in most Melanesian countries, including Vanuatu and Fiji, we have it as a savoury dish.

Could people replicate anything that your communities are doing?
Yesterday, I watched a clip of a lady cooking in a banana leaf as a new thing. We do this every day, using a banana or sago leaf – that's packaging for us! So, the world can learn from us more. We can help you identify with your natural environment, how to connect with nature. Our connection with the land is spiritual. If you don't have land here, you don't have anything; you lack identity, your place.

Shiralee Saul

Smallholder – Portugal

Based in sunny Portugal, Shiralee grows a wide range of exciting crops that are suitable for the drier, hotter areas of our temperate world. This also comes with challenges from a changing climate, including wild fires, drought and shifting seasons...

Can you tell me about where you live?
Central Portugal has hot dry summers and frosty wet winters. We are on a rocky, south-facing hillside with some flat terraces, overall with generally poor, dusty soil. In the fields of the village on the other side of the hill, with a small river and continuously cultivated *hortas* (large veg plots), everything grows earlier, more lushly and more productively.

Please can you tell me about your experiences growing olives and making your own olive oil?
We have about 20 productive olive trees and another five seedlings. We get between 13 and 25 litres of olive oil a year; the difference is because each tree only has a crop every two years as a result of the way we harvest. Also, many of the trees were damaged in a devastating forest fire in 2017 and some are still struggling. I usually preserve a few litres of olives for cooking and making tapenade.

Is pressing olive oil something anyone could do at home?
It is possible to home-extract the oil, but it's a laborious and relatively inefficient process. Here, there are many *lagars*, which are olive presses. We take ours along to a traditional cold press with the harvests of other friends, so we have sufficient to make a pressing, about half a tonne, with chemical-free olives. The pressed residue is used to fuel the steam engine that crushes the olives with big stone grinders and then squeezes and filters the crushed pulp through straw mats. It is always delicious!

Has climate change affected crops like olives and almonds?
Every year, everyone comments that the harvest seems to be getting earlier and earlier, and the oldest people remember when they often picked in January. Now it is usually October when the olives are ready for harvest. Winters are warmer and wetter too, and this has impacted the fertility of fruit trees, with early-flowering almonds and plums becoming less productive as the flowers are washed off the trees by heavy rains without being pollinated. Asian hornets have devastated the local bee populations too, so there are far fewer to do the pollinating. We have no plums at all this year [2025], as birds or squirrels got the few we had, and I'll be surprised if we get more than a handful of almonds from our three trees. Especially as the woodpeckers seem to love them. The warmer winters mean that we have almost no hazelnuts either, though the trees grow really well here.

Left Shiralee on her terraced smallholding surrounded by olive and fruit trees suitable for the drier summers in Portugal.

Do you grow other perennial edible crops?
Chestnuts and walnuts also grow well locally, though our young trees are yet to produce crops. We currently gather them from some huge old trees at a nearby river beach. We get about 20kg of chestnuts and a couple of kilograms of walnuts each autumn.

Other fruit trees that do well on our land include grapes, Japanese loquats, *medhronos* (from strawberry trees), *feijoas* (pineapple guavas) quince, pomegranates, figs, pears, peaches and citrus fruits. We have lemons, limes, blood oranges, tangerines, and sweet and bitter. I have had mixed success with cherries, apricots and apples. Some years we get a few, but in others nothing. We also get a few tamarillos, passion fruit and guavas most years, but the winter cold tends to knock them about badly.

Kangaroo apples thrive, prickly pears do well, and I grow a range of quasi-perennials such as *tremoços* (the beans from lupins), grass peas, Jerusalem artichokes and actual artichokes, walking stick kale, chard, New Zealand spinach (*Tetragonia tetragonioides*) and other self-seeded veggies. I harvest nigella seeds and linseed from self-seeded plants. We also have a couple of asparagus plants, but have only had a few spears so far. I think they need far more watering than I can give them. And I encourage the edible weeds like nettles, a local wild onion, wild strawberry, chicory, purslane (*Portulaca oleracea*), fat hen and evening primrose.

Above Annual poppies bring a sweep of colour to lower perennial herbs under the trees, including rosemary, curry plant and sage.

June

Home gardener – Yorkshire

Our neighbour June is a keen gardener who started growing perennial edibles during Covid lockdowns high on the Pennine Hills of Yorkshire...

When did you first get into growing food?
I've always loved gardening, but I've been disabled for 30 years, and I can do little physically myself. During Covid in 2020, especially early on when nobody knew what was happening, we saw our lack of food security and how we're not at all self-sufficient as a country. It made me think we should all be growing food. During Covid my husband Jon and our son Rowan were at home, so I took advantage of that to barrow soil around and dig to make beds.

And you found getting into growing easy and enjoyable by the sound of it?
I love it. I have a lot of help from Jon and I employ someone too, but I like to do what I can myself, such as sowing seeds. Each year in spring, I think, 'I'm not going to be able to manage it' because I'm low on

Below June in her orchard picking red cooking apple 'Monarch', a variety that was popular during the Second World War. To the left is green cooking apple 'Lord Derby'.

energy and there's lots of other things to do. Then seeds start sprouting and things start growing and I think, this is brilliant. I always think I won't manage it, but I do.

Your garden's fantastic, with seedlings everywhere! And lots of perennial edibles...

I tend to have less energy in winter and early spring, and I don't really get going till mid-afternoon most days, so in summer, I come out and do stuff in the evening. I can get a lot more done and the days are in my favour with late evenings. With perennials, even if I haven't done anything, there they are – like these Welsh onions. I've been eating them for ages and I haven't done anything.

How did you get into perennial crops?

I thought perennials would be more sustainable and easier for me to grow. We already had the apple trees, of course, which are perennials, mint, chives, a few herbs. We store fruit in the shed, and it lasts okay. Fruit trees take a bit of looking after – against canker especially, which likes cold and wet. I'm always cutting canker off, but the trees survive if we keep on top of it.

Which are your favourite perennial crops?

Welsh onions and the 'Perutile' onions really look after themselves. Onion greens are much better than actual onions. If you cut them and leave an inch above ground, they grow again. Daubenton's kale we pick through the winter. In spring it goes mad and with loads of lovely young greens. It's supposed to last 10 years – one died from black spot disease and the wind got another – but it's very easy to grow from side cuttings. Sea kale is beautiful. Last year they had masses of flowers, but smaller leaves to eat. A beautiful show, but this year I might take some of the flowers off to put energy into the leaves. Sea kale's got thicker leaves like cabbage and a stronger flavour. Rhubarb, I've got 'Victoria' and 'Timperley Early'. And our gooseberries and white currants have been here longer than us, and we've been here since 1989!

Above June's Welsh onions and sea kale make for a strikingly beautiful combination – in the garden and on the plate!

Have any not worked?

'Nine Star' perennial broccoli was lovely for two years, but a black spot disease finished them off. Skirret I've tried and failed at miserably; the rabbits mainly had it, so that didn't do well. I did try sea beet, which did alright for one year. It has thicker and stronger-flavoured leaves, a bit like perennial spinach. Sorrel is better though; it tastes lemony, so nice in a salad. I'm making sure we don't pull that up with the weeds.

A bit of foraging...

Yes, I like wild garlic too, that's always good. I try not to bring anything into the garden, to be self-sufficient. I don't completely succeed, but I start seeds with half collected molehill soil and half garden compost. Occasionally, some little plant comes up from our compost, like strawberries. I've got a compost avocado plant inside too, an absolute beauty. Of course, tomatoes and potatoes, they're all perennials, just not in our climate.

Nick Dent

Professional gardener – Yorkshire

After buying a steep triangle of unwanted land covered in brambles, professional gardener Nick is starting a food forest for the community.

Have you always been a gardener?
I left school and went into accountancy, but it wasn't for me. I worked with the Scottish Wildlife Trust for a year doing habitat surveys, where I gained my knowledge of wild plants, then I pursued horticultural qualifications and became a head gardener. When we moved here I got a job at a hospice, developing the garden over 17 years and creating a vegetable garden, orchard and ornamental beds.

Above Nick on his land shortly after buying it; it's a blank canvas he and the community are planting with perennial crops for the future.

Can you tell me about your new plot?
The idea is for it to be an experimental site; it's two-thirds of an acre. I'm trying to get everything free, so there's less pressure if plants get eaten or die. I've started watering a little to see plants through dry spells, otherwise I leave them alone. People really overwater and overfeed things. It's better to see what nature's doing, and try to emulate that. We need major changes if we have any chance of tackling climate change, and see how few resources we can use. Stress-testing plants now is going to be important for the future. If something doesn't make it through a dry period, you have to write it off. Otherwise, how will we cope with longer, drier spells?

Why did you buy this triangle of land?
It's partly because I wanted to do something to acknowledge Jules, my late wife. Although we weren't deeply involved in this particular community until after her passing, we took part in other hospice projects and Jules had her own too. She liked that sort of thing, so it seemed a good use of some of the inherited money. I also always liked the idea of having some land and growing food.

And you're thinking of using the land for the community?
Yeah, people walking through might stop and sit. If people are working on it, others can chat and get involved. Eventually, everyone will be able to help themselves to food, encouraging foraging. I also want seating spaces where we can gather and enjoy workshops.

When did you become interested in forest gardening?
I started deep diving into permaculture, including forest gardening, after becoming vegan and thinking about truly sustainable methods and alternatives to animal protein. I like the idea of the layered system, maximizing the area rather than growing one crop in strips. On a larger scale, huge monoculture fields aren't very resilient. I like the idea of working with nature – forest gardening can be similar to organising an ornamental border.

Do you carry veganism into gardening and are there challenges, or is it easier?
Even when I wasn't a vegan I gardened organically. At the hospice, because I was there for such a long time, I managed to get the balance right. There were all sorts of animals living on site that controlled what

Below Volunteers helping plant an edible hedge of hazelnut, elderflower, crab apple, blackthorn, rowan and dog rose to make jams, cordial and chutney.

Right Hostas are one of the main perennial crops Nick is planning to fill the space as they grow especially well in the area.

people class as pests, like slugs. All wildlife has a role; it's about seeing them within an ecosystem. They might eat your plants because you've put something tasty where they live. Trying to find good veganic compost without animal products can be difficult to get hold of. We had a good composting system at the hospice and a supply of leaf mould, so I started experimenting with making my own composts.

What plants have you been adding?
I've been focusing on edible flowering plants. I was surprised how nice hostas are to eat, so I'll be splitting and spreading those. And I love wild garlic, which I've used for years to make pesto. It can be quite aggressive though, once established. I also want to focus on nuts, especially walnuts.

Could others replicate what you're doing, either on their own or collectively?
Yes, others locally have created a market garden on a larger scale. There seems to be a movement for this sort of thing. It's nice to think of gardens that will last, and to do this, you need to involve a community. We come together and make friends through the garden. It's permaculture principles again; you're more resilient as an individual if you have a community around you.

qm'qant | Kaeloni

Traditional Ecological Knowledge Keeper – British Columbia, Canada

On a trip to British Columbia I visited first nation Indian communities in old growth forests. It's hard not to feel drawn to their historic connections with nature. Here, I met qm'qant, who explained the importance of perennials both historically and today.

Please can you tell me a bit more about you and your community?
Wai', my name is *qm'qamt*, meaning 'calm'. My given name is Kaeloni. I was born and raised in *sn'pinktn*, also known as Penticton, which loosely translates as 'a place to stay forever'. Nestled beautifully between two bodies of water, Okanagan Lake and Skaha Lake, we are lucky enough to experience all four seasons. We were semi-nomadic people and moved around with the seasons. I am a proud two-spirit member of the Penticton Indian Band, born female, and embrace my female energy, but my spirit also encompasses a male spirit or masculine energy, and they both flow through me. From a traditional standpoint, two-spirit people were highly regarded as medicine people and healers, offering trusted guidance.

Below Saskatoon berries of *Amelanchier alnifolia* are sweet with a hint of marzipan that grow on a medium size flowering and very hardy tree.

How do you view nature and your relationship with it?
I view my relationship with nature almost like a symbiotic relationship. I know nature would thrive without humans, but without nature my life and lifestyle do not exist. My connection with nature is as deeply rooted as indigenous grasses growing near a marsh or bog. The deeper the roots, the more water retention you achieve and the more the surrounding area flourishes. My connection with nature flourished when I decided to go back to school, learning about Environmental Studies and Natural Resources. It helped bridge the gap between traditional knowledge and modern science. I studied many things, from soil compositions to silvics and dendrology. I learned that every part of the Earth has cycles. Soil, for example, usually contains leaf litter, fibre, humus. Layers of decomposing organics that eventually turn into 'black gold'. The trees also have life cycles, and mother trees send proteins to their saplings, so they can thrive. Mycelium networks connect all of this. I was brought up to understand that everything we see, everything on Earth, is connected. In Nsyilxcen the word is *tmixw*. *Tmixw* is the earth, the plants, the animals, everything that walks this planet. We are all connected.

Has your community's use of plants for food and other reasons changed in today's world?
There was a time when our community was extremely reliant on plants, and the cycles of the seasons. Buttercups tell us spring is around the corner. Tule from sedge plants (Carex) was used to make mats for temporary shelters through the summer and early autumn. When the arrowleaf balsamroot dies, it's time to start hunting. Saskatoon berries are wildly

Above Kaeloni lives between the Okanagan and Skaha lakes in western Canada, surrounded by land from which to gather wild crops.

abundant; soap berries and huckleberries are also enjoyed. Many of our berries were dried to sustain us through winter. Our people also foraged for bitterroot, which was preserved to consume during the long, dark winter for vitamins and nutrients. Stinging nettles were harvested and collected to treat rheumatoid arthritis.

Do any uses continue today and have any stopped?
We're doing our best to relearn and preserve the traditional uses of plants. Due to the residential schooling forced on Indigenous communities across Canada, many hurdles stop members of our community from learning and foraging for our traditional foods and medicines. However, I started a new job with Penticton Indian Band Health Department and have recently learned of many programmes directed at on-the-land learning, as well as harvesting/foraging. It's a chance for us to connect with our ancestors who practised these methods before us. Part of my job is also teaching food preservation, such as canning and dehydrating fruits and berries, so we can regain this knowledge and practice.

Today, are there any perennial crops you or others in your community grow, nurture or forage for food?
Our community has been nurturing a community garden. I'd like to see crops of our berries, planted between the schools, daycare and health centre, for the children to learn their growing cycles: saskatoon berries, soap berries, redcurrants, and huckleberries. At the end of the growing cycle we can all gather and forage from these berry crops, and the children can learn how to preserve them and what the berries look like, from flowers to fruit.

Professor Megan Povey

Food physicist – University of Leeds

I visited Professor Megan Povey at the University of Leeds for a tour of the School of Food Science and Nutrition labs in order to understand the processes that give information on what's in our food.

How can people at home work out what's in their food?
With a great deal of difficulty, to be quite honest. Our food analysis labs use various ways of finding nutritional components in food. I would never give nutrition advice because people are so different; as a diabetic, I'm managing my blood sugar through diet, but there's no one type of diabetes and there's no one nutritional guide.

What are the main components people should look for?
Fundamentals are protein, carbohydrates, fats, minerals, vitamins, phytochemicals and water – then there's fibre, which is not simple or trivial at all because not all fibres are equal. There is a huge nutritional difference between a raw fruit and a juice. Juicing breaks down fibre, releasing sugar in the stomach. While whole, fibre slows release to the intestine, where fungi and bacteria consume the sugar and use it to break up lipids – the fats – producing nutrition much more slowly and effectively. Not all fat is bad by the way – unrefined fat is good.

Fibre sounds important for different reasons to what I'd expected...
Yes, fibre is the scaffolding of the plant, binding the cells and changing the way we digest food. Where food components are delivered in the digestive system makes a massive difference. Importantly, fibre will arrive in the small intestine, where bacteria and fungi can digest some of it but not all. For example, if you've ever eaten whole sweetcorn, it generally goes straight through. The interior of the sweetcorn is a highly digestible starch called amylopectin but because it's encapsulated within the seed, it might not be digested.

Can you explain what polyphenols are?
Apples have one of the highest counts of the polyphenol quercetin – very powerful, long-lasting antioxidants – so are very good for your cardiovascular system. One a day helps keep the doctor away. Polyphenols are really good nutritionally, but whether they survive being juiced is another matter. If you take an apple and grate it, the flesh will go brown within minutes because it's so easily oxidised. Whereas if it's bound in the fibre and the cell structure is entire, then that package stays intact.

Does freshness of food affect nutrition?
It depends on the food, processing and preserving techniques. To preserve food, we want to manage the process of natural enzymes breaking down cells (senescence), such as by salting, freezing, drying and canning. Canning is very effective, but food has to be cooked first. So long as cells are undamaged, such as by not mashing, you'll usually get a longer shelf life.

Will food science change what we eat in the future?
It will as long as it's in the hands of people and scientists and not corporations. We have to change what we eat for two reasons: health and sustainability. Ultra-processed foods in particular are causing serious health problems, and agriculture is a big source of greenhouse gases being pumped into the atmosphere. But the issue is the food industry exists to make a profit and for no other reason in my view.

I've always thought of food as nutrition. If only the world would go back to focusing on cultivating fruit as natural sweets, helping us shift away from unhealthy foods!
A healthy diet would transform lives but when you go into the supermarket, what's on sale to tempt you at the checkout? Sweets. In my garden, we've got blackcurrants, blackberries, plums, apples, pears, and wild-growing Japanese wine berries. They're only little, but you get so much fruit on them. And I've recently discovered, as a diabetic, thanks to sugars being locked in their fibre, I can eat fruit till it comes out of my ears.

Opposite A large range of different tools and techniques are used for assessing the different components of food.

Below Professor Megan Povey is a physicist who uses novel ultrasound and acoustics to study food, specialising in the role of sound in our appreciation of food.

Nutrition

Below is a simplified overview of some of the main nutrients our bodies need and how we currently understand their benefits.

COMPONENT	ABOUT	PLANT SOURCES
Macronutrients		
Carbohydrates – Sugars – Starch – Dietary fibre (see prebiotics below)	Includes simple sugars like glucose and fructose, plus complex sugars locked in starch and fibre. Around half of our energy comes from carbohydrates. Dietary fibre is an important component of our diets which we obtain from plants and is not digested in the stomach or small intestine. This keeps our digestive system healthy and carries digestible components through our entire gut biome, feeding microorganisms in our intestines that make plant components accessible to our bodies, releasing energy slowly through the day.	Wholegrains, potatoes, legumes, rice, fruit, Chinese artichokes, sunchokes, sweet chestnut, pine nuts, monkey puzzle, dahlia tubers, chicken of the woods and jelly ear fungi
Proteins	Proteins are used by almost every part of the body, from bones and muscle to hair. In developed countries it's easy to access enough protein, but in underdeveloped countries many people face a protein deficiency. In developed countries people may need less protein than we think, and it's known that protein obtained from plants is good for our long-term health and the prevention of serious diseases. Plant proteins have a lower impact on wildlife and emissions.	Beans (including edamame beans), lentils, chickpeas, nuts, quinoa, seeds, mushrooms
Good fats (unsaturated fats: monounsaturated and polyunsaturated)	Fat can be good for us, giving us energy, as long as we eat the right types in the right quantities. Unsaturated fats are good for our bodies. They help maintain good cholesterol, while reducing bad cholesterol, and are necessary for us to absorb vitamins A, D and E. Saturated and trans fats, on the other hand, are bad in large quantities, and found in the likes of butter, coconut oil, margarine, fatty red meat, processed and deep-fried food.	Walnuts, almonds, cashew nuts, seeds and seed oils, olive oil, avocado
Micronutrients – Minerals (naturally occurring, inorganic)		
Calcium	Builds bones and healthy teeth, regulates muscle contractions, including of the heart, and is important for blood clotting	Leafy greens like kale, bread
Chromium	Helps the body metabolise fats, carbohydrates and proteins, in particular to help insulin work better.	Nuts and cereal grains

COMPONENT	ABOUT	PLANT SOURCES
Copper	Essential for the production of red and white blood cells, triggering the release of iron to form haemoglobin.	Nuts
Iodine	Important for the formation of thyroid hormones that help keep cells and the metabolic rate healthy.	Cereals and grains (but depends on soil in which plants grown)
Iron	Needed to make red blood cells.	Nuts, kidney and edamame beans, leafy greens, dried fruit
Magnesium	Turns food into energy and contributes to bone health.	Spinach, nuts, wholemeal bread
Manganese	Makes and activates enzymes in the body – enzymes are proteins that conduct chemicals reactions, such as breaking down food.	Nuts, green vegetables, cereals, bread
Molybdenum	Activates proteins to help the enzymes that repair and make genetic material.	Crops growing above ground, (photosynthetic parts)
Phosphorus	Builds strong bones and teeth, and releases energy from food.	Bread, brown rice, oats
Potassium	Helps heart muscle to work properly, and controls the balance of fluids in the body.	Bananas, broccoli, parsnips, Brussels sprouts, beans and pulses, nuts and seeds
Selenium	Contributes to the proper working of the immune system, supports reproduction, and prevents cell and tissue damage.	Brazil nuts, mushrooms
Sodium chloride (salt)	Balances the level of fluids in the body and to digest food.	Naturally in all food (we usually eat too much)
Zinc	Makes new cells and enzymes, processes carbohydrates, fat and protein in food, and heals wounds.	Bread, cereals (e.g. wheatgerm)
Vitamins (naturally occurring organic micronutrients)		
Vitamin A	Needed for the immune system and vision in dim light, plus keeps skin and some internal linings of the body healthy.	Carrots, broccoli, squash, most perennial leafy greens, apricots, mango (See also Carotenoids)
B-vitamins (including folate) – thiamine (vitamin B1) – riboflavin (vitamin B2) – niacin (vitamin B3) – pantothenic acid (vitamin B5) – biotin (vitamin B7) – folate (vitamin B9) and folic acid – cobalamin (vitamin B12)	B-vitamins are a group of water-soluble chemical compounds and should be treated as separate vitamins. They have wide-ranging biological uses, including for our immune and nervous systems, releasing energy from food, and storing energy in our bodies. Folate helps the body repair cells and form red blood cells; folic acid is the human-made form.	Wholegrains, beans, lentils, chickpeas, bread, oats, nuts and seeds, leafy greens, brassicas, peas, mushrooms, fruit **Note:** Vitamin B12 is mainly found in meat and dairy. products, so vegans may need a supplement.

COMPONENT	ABOUT	PLANT SOURCES
Vitamin C	Known as ascorbic acid. Helps protect cells and with wound healing. Maintains a healthy body.	Brassicas, leafy greens, potatoes, apples, berries, citrus
Vitamin D	Regulates calcium and phosphorus in the body to keep bones, teeth and muscles healthy.	Sunlight, UV-exposed mushrooms, supplements
Vitamin E	Maintains a healthy immune system, skin and eyes.	Nuts and seeds, plant oils, wheatgerm
Vitamin K	A group of vitamins that helps blood clotting and wound healing.	Leafy greens, brassicas, plant oils, cereal grains
Other Beneficial Compounds		
Carotenoids	Show strong antioxidant activity, helping prevent chronic diseases. Help with macular degeneration and cataracts, and protect against sunburn-related disorders. Some carotenoids are known as provitamin A carotenoids, which the body converts into vitamin A. A good example is beta-carotene.	Leafy greens, carrots, sweet potatoes, pumpkin, dandelion
Glucosinolates	A group of plant chemicals made of sulphur- and nitrogen-containing compounds found in the Brassicaceae family. They are thought to help our bodies detoxify and regulate inflammation, reducing the risk of serious disease such as diabetes, cancer and heart disease.	Brassicas
Phytosterols	Plant compounds similar to cholesterol that can significantly help lower blood cholesterol.	Vegetable oils, nuts and seeds, beans, lentils
Polyphenols	A large group of thousands of compounds found in plants that science is just starting to understand. It is thought polyphenols reduce inflammation and the risk of serious neurodegenerative diseases as well as heart disease.	Leafy greens, dark berries, olives and extra-virgin olive oil, apples, herbs, teas, chestnuts, almonds, hazelnuts, tempeh
Prebiotics	Prebiotics are types of fibre that our bodies can't break down, but microbes in our gut microbiome can. They are thought to improve the intestinal absorption of nutrients, help manage blood sugar, and reduce the risk of colon cancer. (Probiotics are microorganisms that are able to break down prebiotics.)	Sunchoke, Chinese artichoke, asparagus, beans, lentils, onion, garlic, bananas

Further reading

EDIBLE PERENNIALS

Agroforestry Research Trust (agroforestry.co.uk)
Non-profit agroforestry and perennial crop nursery, research and education

Chris Bowers (chrisbowers.co.uk)
Nursery specialising in fruit and nuts

Crûg Farm Plants (crug-farm.co.uk)
Nursery exploring new plant species for ornamental use

Florida Fruit Geek (floridafruitgeek.com)
Information on unusual fruit and nut crops in Florida, USA

Incredible Vegetables (incrediblevegetables.co.uk)
Nursery specialising in perennial crops

Kew Science (kew.org)
Non-profit botanical research

Otter Farm (otterfarm.co.uk)
Nursery specialising in edibles, especially perennials

Pine Island Nursery (pineislandnursery.com)
Nursery specialising in fruit and nuts for Florida, USA

Plants for a Future (pfaf.org)
Non-profit database of perennial and annual crops

Royal Horticultural Society (rhs.org.uk)
Non-profit horticulture research and education

RV Roger Nursery (rvroger.co.uk)
Nursery with expertise in fruit and nuts for colder climates

The Citrus Centre (citruscentre.co.uk)
Nursery specialising in citrus plants

Victoriana Nursery Gardens (victoriananursery.co.uk)
Nursery specialising in all edibles

Walnut Trees Company (walnuttrees.co.uk)
Nursery specialising in walnut cultivars, plus other nuts, fruit and olives

FUNGI IDENTIFICATION BOOKS

Geoffrey Kibby, *Mushrooms and Toadstools of Britain and Ireland* (Volumes 1–4), Geoffrey Kibby (Privately Published), 2017–2024
Encyclopaedias to identify all fungi imagineable. Does not focus on edibility guidance.

Roger Philips, *Mushrooms*, Macmillan, 2006
Easy-to-understand edible fungi guide

FOOD COMPOSITION DATABASES

British Nutrition Foundation (nutrition.org.uk)

European Food Safety Authority (efsa.europa.eu)
Food composition database

Food and Agriculture Organization of the United Nations (fao.org)

National Health Service (nhs.uk/conditions/vitamins-and-minerals)
Guide to vitamins and minerals

Quadram Institute (quadram.ac.uk/UKfoodcomposition)
UK food composition database

US Department of Agriculture (fdc.nal.usda.gov)
Food composition database

World Health Organisation (who.int/teams/nutrition-and-food-safety)
Nutrition and food safety department

PEER-REVIEWED SCIENTIFIC REPORTS AND JOURNALS

I have included only nutritional information from trusted food-composition databases and peer-reviewed scientific research. Peer-reviewed work is produced by qualified specialists and checked by other specialists – often scientists in universities or research institutions – before being published on their websites or on aggregators such as:

British Ecological Society (besjournals.onlinelibrary.wiley.com)

Emerald Insight (emerald.com)

Europe PMC (europepmc.org)

Google Scholar (scholar.google.com)

Multidisciplinary Digital Publishing Institute (mdpi.com)

PubMed (pubmed.ncbi.nlm.nih.gov)

Research Gate (researchgate.net)

Science Direct (sciencedirect.com)

Springer Nature Link (link.springer.com)

Acknowledgements

Julie Bailey, Heather Bradbury, Caroline West. Austin Taylor, Jacky Ferneyhough, Amanda Keyte and Ella Corsan, thank you for believing in *Grower Gatherer*, for your guidance and working tirelessly to bring it into the world so beautifully. Dotti Irving, thank you for bursting into my life with your wisdom, humour and unrelenting support – you helped me remember why I love writing. To my partner Christopher Lyon Anderson thank you as always for your guidance and patience. I'm grateful to everyone who has spoken generously to me over the years about your food growing experiences: Nick Dent, David and Anna Gibson, Jo Gorner, Kaeloni, Prisilla Manove, Professor Megan Povey, June, Shiralee Saul, Jenny Slaughter, Darren Turpin, Dan Ryan, Caren Thompson and John Butterworth. Sally Hayes and Ben Plumpton, thank you for passing on your knowledge and for your inspiring determination. This book is for all nature-led growers and farmers who feed our world.

Photo credits

Bloomsbury Publishing would like to thank the following for providing photographs and for permission to reproduce copyright material within this book. While every effort has been made to trace and acknowledge all copyright holders, we would like to apologise for any errors or omissions, and invite readers to inform us so that corrections can be made to future editions.

Key: T = top; L = left; R = right; B = bottom.

Abbreviated photo agency names: A = Alamy; G = Getty Images; iS = iStock; SS = Shutterstock.

36: SS/sanddebeautheil. **46:** SS/simona pavan. **47:** SS/Orest Iyzhechka. **52:** G/SUNGMOON HAN. **53:** A/piemags/nature. **63:** SS/Victoria Moloman. **81T:** SS/Kathy D. Reasor. **84:** SS/Macarena Assiego. **85T:** SS/ShotPrime Studio. **85B:** SS/Gurcharan Singh. **88:** SS/Olha Solodenko. **90:** SS/thekovtun. **91:** SS/Voss Tau. **92:** SS/darynahuz. **108:** SS/Magdanatka. **109:** SS/tamu1500. **111:** SS/Lubos Chlubny. **112:** SS/Adria Black. **116:** SS/OkiWorks Studio. **128:** A/Deborah Vernon. **129:** SS/Valentyn Volkov. **131:** SS/Luca love photo. **132:** SS/Ildi Papp. **133B:** SS/LuanRS. **133T:** SS/Anthony King Nature. **134:** SS/Dream79. **135:** SS/vallefrias. **138:** Jenny Slaughter. **142:** Christopher Lyon Anderson. **153:** SS/Stephen Farhall. **160, 161R:** A/piemags/nature. **162:** SS/Pat Moore. **163:** iS/geoleo. 164: SS/Kati Maria. **165:** SS/adamikral. **170:** SS/Sonny Vermeer. **171:** SS/Ninevija. **172:** SS/Ikhsansaputra. **173:** SS/Jack Hong. **174, 175:** Shiralee Saul. **178, 179B:** Nick Dent. **179T:** SS/Vilda.S. **180:** SS/Jennifer de Graaf. **181:** Jenny Popoff.

Index

Bold type indicates the main pages for that plant or plant group.

S

T

V

W

Y